A Soldier's Message

General Louis-Gaston de Sonis

A
Soldier's Message

by D.C.N.

A REFLECTION BOOK

Comet Press Books   New York

NIHIL OBSTAT
Bede Babo, O. S. B.
       Censor Librorum
Paterson, May 4, 1958

IMPRIMATUR
✠ James A. McNulty
Bishop of Paterson
May 6, 1958

To

MARY IMMACULATE

Queen of Mount Carmel

To commemorate the Centenary of Her appearance

at the Grotto of Lourdes—

this life of Miles Christi is lovingly dedicated

with an ardent prayer

that She who was so specially his Mother under both these

titles may make the Hero of these pages

a light burning and shining

in the darkness of Communism and Materialism

that overshadows the earth. . . .

Acknowledgments

The author wishes to express thanks to the following people and sources: Beauchesnes et ses Fils for permission to quote from *Sonis* by Rev. Albert Bessières, S. J.—a permission fully utilized; the Rev. Rémy Thevert, pastor of the Church of the Sacred Heart at Loigny-la-Bataille for permission to use his brochure *Sonis-Loigny* and for his cooperation in furnishing information; the Discalced Carmelite Nuns of Verdun for permission to quote from *Germaine de Sonis* (a biography of their foundress) by André Trannoy, and for their kind assistance and interest.

Further thanks are extended to all who have made this book possible.

D. C. N.

Note: The use of the word "saint" or any other similar expression in this book is in no way intended to anticipate the judgments reserved to the Holy Catholic Church alone.

Contents

Preface

A strange, new militancy seems to have taken hold of the people since Father Peyton began the Crusade of the Rosary. Many, many people stopped being anxious about the cold war. They felt that new things were happening and that new hopes were born. Then, in a way that no one had ever imagined, Communism started going to pieces. Communists dealt themselves the severest blows to their own system and its ideologies. In the great captive world of red silence, tongues were loosed. Throughout the world, Communist Parties began to break up. Then, an unbelievable Marian year thrilled Poland, brought it to the feet of Our Lady of Czestochowa; the Cardinal-Primate, brought back from his prison by the prime-minister, returned to Warsaw on the feast of Christ the King. After that, the Hungarian happenings shook the world, and no one has the faintest idea of what will happen next.

Now, a cloistered nun, a Carmelite, gives America the biography of a cavalry officer who, above all, was Christ's own knight. *Miles Christi!* General Gaston de Sonis seems to be as universal as the modern world. Born in the West Indies, on the island of Guadeloupe, Sonis was a French officer who fought most of his battles in North Africa. He was pious enough so that he could write: "I believe I did not lose sight of the presence of God for a single instant during that terrible day." That was at the Battle of Solferino, on June 24, 1859, when he remained in the saddle for twenty-four hours without food and drink; he later was given the Legion of Honor for his courage on that day. Our Carmelite, who draws the conclusion that it takes a contemplative to be a good soldier, has a few strong words on the necessity of contemplation in the modern world.

He is the soldier of desperate situations. Over and over again, you see him pulling victory out of nothingness with the ease of a magician. As he is winning a new battle, his preceding ones are discussed in the seminaries, for the edification of the young men who are getting ready for the priesthood. Sonis had six sons. He wanted them to be soldiers or priests. None became priests—all went to the military academy; one enlisted with the Papal Zouaves before he was fifteen.

He was nearly always assigned to dangerous missions; from 1856, when he took part in his first African battle, until 1870, when he was disabled on the battlefield of Loigny, we find him nearly always at the front. He is perhaps more amazing in his acceptance of daily responsibility. Financially, he is a poor man. His only income is an officer's pay. On that, he brings up twelve children. His wife, often separated from her husband by battle, is as heroic as he. By a little political maneuvering, he could easily have climbed the ladder of human success. He was pushed by nasty politics from one unpleasant post to another, until that awful November, 1880, when he was asked to expel the Religious.

Sonis then resigned: "In selecting the military career, I was willing to sacrifice my life, but not my honor. If I have nothing else to give my children when I die, I want at least to leave them a name that is honored and respected."

He died on August 15, 1887. Now, his cause of beatification has been introduced, and one wonders if this soldier, who is a contemplative, and the very embodiment of the message of Fatima—to sanctify oneself in one's own state of life—is not going to be the military saint who, after Saint George, Saint Victor, Saint Dimitri of Thessalonica, Saint Henry of Germany, Saint Louis of France, is called to carry to victory the banner of Our Lady. And that may perhaps be the reason why his biographer obtained the cooperation of the secular clergy and asked a Jesuit of the Eastern Rite to write a short preface to her book. All together unto victory. . . .

Joseph Ledit, S.J.

Montréal
May 13, 1957

The Question

⟋⟍⟋⟍⟋⟍⟋⟍⟋⟍⟋⟍⟋⟍⟋⟍⟋⟍⟋⟍⟋⟍⟋⟍⟋⟍⟋⟍⟋⟍⟋⟍⟋⟍⟋⟍⟋⟍⟍

"The Jews sent from Jerusalem priests and levites to John, to ask him: Who art thou? . . . art thou Elias . . . ? Art thou the prophet . . . ? Who art thou that we may give an answer to them that sent us? What sayest thou of thyself?" *(John I, 19-22)*

In selecting this Gospel passage at the opening of her year, the Church does not intend merely to set before her children a scene that took place beyond the Jordan over 1900 years ago. She wants us to draw practical lessons from Holy Scripture, which was written for our instruction, and weave them into the very warp and woof of our lives. How shall we do it?

"Tu quis es? Who art thou? When I had finished my prayer, I could not help putting this question to myself: who are you? I then found myself transported to a world without end which, starting from the first days of childhood, brought me to this present day, carried by the hand of this God so good. Who am I to have been stopped at the first years of youth from entering the way that leads to the abyss? We are souls redeemed at the price of a God. We are not only bodies of flesh and clay; we are something great. We are immortal souls."

1

Is this passage taken from the diary of a monk or the private musings of a cloistered nun in her cell? No. It is quoted from a letter of a soldier of 39, written in his tent which was his only protection from the scorching African sun, and whose cloister was the vast sands of the Sahara. It was the third Sunday of Advent of the year 1864, and two days before, he had welcomed into the world his ninth child!

There will not be many pages to separate the back from the front cover of this book and the chapters will be short. The purpose of this little volume is to introduce to the people of America the hero of its story, and as introductions are brief, so will this story be brief. Battles should be recounted by soldiers, so the battles will not be described. Picturesque descriptions of places will be omitted as these places cannot be visited, and you will not be asked to spend your precious time reading the fancies of someone's imagination. The subject matter would easily lend itself to a beautiful story clothed in modern dramatic style, but do not look for this treatment either. What, then? Some plain, bare facts, and wherever they can be given in the words of the subject of this story these will be given preference. A bibliography will be found at the back of the book for those desirous of more information. The impossibility to meet the requirements gave birth to the present book rather than to a translation.

When the Church raises someone to her altars, it is to place before her children a model to be imitated, an example to be followed in circumstances similar to our own; someone who has a message to give us. In our own day, we have been given examples from every walk of life, every condition, age and sex: a sainted Pope and a simple parish priest; learned theologians and unlettered children (who were simple enough, however, to understand the message the Queen of Heaven brought for the whole world) ; men and women who founded religious congregations, and humble servants of the Lord, hidden in the ranks.

Never, as in the present century, have "wars and rumors of wars" so shaken the world. Thinkers even outside the Church realize the struggle today is not that of nation against nation, East against West, so much as Communism against the Catholic Church—Satan against God. Do we not need the example of a soldier, a man of arms, in these turbulent days when one cannot take a thoughtful breath without scenting gunpowder, when military training is calling forth the youth of every nation? Is there not a vacant place for such a one in the long ranks of haloed heroes?

And so it is Sonis, the man, we introduce to you, Sonis, who is no less the hero of the home and the family than of the battlefield, Sonis who attained sanctity by heroic fidelity to the duties of his state in life—the intransigent son of the Church who broke his sword rather than commit sacrilege, the father of a large family when it was not fashionable to have many children, the self-sacrificing husband who knew no joy apart from his wife, the noble who courted Lady Poverty, the soldier of faultless patriotism— yes, General Gaston de Sonis is all this. He is an example for men and women of all conditions and professions in the world, and not less for the priest or cloistered religious who is striving to be an *alter Christus*. He has been termed a model for Catholic Action. Those who are devoting themselves to fight Communism will find in him a leader, a defender, an advocate.

In the prayer composed for the Year of Mary, 1954, our

3

Holy Father, Pope Pius XII, reminded us that "the nations are members of one family." His Holiness has repeated this thought many times since. It is not the unity of Communism (which is, in reality, tyranny), but, rather, the oneness of Christ's prayer at the Last Supper—one brotherhood respecting the rights and individuality of others. It was to be the hallmark of His disciples: "By this shall all men know you are my disciples, if you have love one for another." If we all were to strive to consider other nations as "members of one family," we would not be so much at sea in our approach to the problem of world peace. If we would pay attention to all that our Holy Father is saying to us, and pray to understand, and try to absorb his teaching, we would arrive at lasting peace. So varied are the groups His Holiness addresses and the topics discussed that one is reminded of King Solomon. Modern scientific discoveries have brought our white robed Father to us into our very homes. May we not give occasion to the Queen of Saba who "came from the ends of the earth to hear the wisdom of Solomon" to rise in judgment against our generation! Behold, we have here a greater than Solomon in our holy Vicar of Jesus Christ.

The world is caught in death-like coldness because hell has swept it with its blasts of hate. But what is the hatred of a million hells compared to the infinite love of our God? When Our Lord gazed over the heads of His Apostles and looked down the avenues of time, of all the evils He saw, He mentioned only one. He knew if that one were corrected, all could be corrected. "Because evil hath abounded, the charity of many shall grow cold." The devotion to the Sacred Heart was kept till the world had grown cold in love, and when the fullness of time had come, it was to the "Eldest Daughter" of the Church,

France, that the sacred deposit was confided. That was in the latter half of the seventeenth century, Saint Margaret Mary Alacoque of the Visitation being the humble instrument. When Our Lord wanted to complete these revelations, He chose another cloistered daughter, Sister Josefa Menendez, religious of the Society of the Sacred Heart. To her He confided His Message of Love for the world. This was in 1922-23. "I have come to cast fire on the earth and what will I but that it be kindled?" There is the Blue Army, the Legion of Mary, but an army is made up of many divisions. Why can there not be a "sacred battalion," an élite troop, with the mission of carrying the fire of the Sacred Heart of Jesus into the very heart of Communism? Like so many atoms, the members would release the energy of His pent-up Love and hurl the whole of its force against the curtain of hate, to forge of the molten iron a bridge of understanding between East and West. What better leader could we have than General Gaston de Sonis who loved so passionately the Heart of His Master and who personifies the very virtues most needed in this crusade against Communism, against Materialism . . . against Satan? What but the heat of God's infinite and merciful Love can melt the Iron Curtain or warm to new life frozen waste-lands?

God seems to have predestined the Order of Carmel, of which General de Sonis was a tertiary member, to a special rôle in the last days. The Carmelites preserve the tradition that their Founder and Leader, the Prophet Elias, will return to earth to fight Antichrist who will kill him. After his body shall have lain for three and a half days unburied, Elias will be raised up and will slay Antichrist. The great mother of Carmel, Saint Teresa of Avila, saw in prophetic vision her children with shining faces battling vigorously, on a large plain, for their Lord and King. It was on July

16th, the Feast of Our Lady of Mount Carmel, that the Immaculate Virgin of Lourdes appeared for the eighteenth and last time to Saint Bernadette. At Her last apparition at Fatima, She was clothed in the Habit of Carmel.

The simple words of Saint Paul, *MILES CHRISTI,* "soldier of Christ," which General de Sonis chose for the inscription on his tomb, sum up the character and the life of this great Frenchman. The Cause for his beatification, which was introduced in 1928, was first in the hands of the Sulpician Fathers at Paris. In 1945, it was given to the Order of Discalced Carmelites. The Ordinary Processes are completed. His writings received Rome's Approbation in May, 1937. The Cause was interrupted by the Second World War. There have been many miracles attributed to the intercession of the Servant of God, but a few more striking ones would hasten the beatification.

"Truly, one does not know what more to admire in General de Sonis," wrote Mgr. Gay. "He had true nobility of soul, boundless courage; he was great in battle; he was no less so in peace. He obeyed as perfectly as he commanded. No success elated him; no difficulty disturbed him, no failure discouraged him. . . . Pious and simple as a child, he was the perfect model of Christian virility. . . . What shall I say of his patience? I think many martyrs who triumph in Heaven did not have to endure so great and such cruel sufferings. His good works will speak his praise better than any panegyric and his greatest miracle will always be the story of his life."

"With desolation is all the land made desolate," lamented Jeremias, "because there is none that considereth in the heart." Would the old Prophet be any happier about the world of our day? We promised not to keep you long, but you are asked to read these pages thoughtfully, because there is a message here for *you*. "Consider in the heart." It is not sufficient to think with one's head. If everyone thought with his heart as well as with his head would there be torture chambers, brain-washings, death-marches, cruelties that make the old Roman martyrology pale? Inhuman cruelties are taking place while these very pages are being written and read, and not on inanimate creatures or dumb beasts, but on throbbing flesh and pulsing blood, on the delicate network of a sensitive nerve system such as you and I have.

CHAPTER I

1825-1844

~~~~~~

It was in 1825, on the 25th of August, the Feast of the great king Saint, Louis IX of France, that Louis-Gaston de Sonis was born at Pointe-à-Pitre, Guadeloupe, an island in the West Indies. His father, Jean-Baptist Charles Gaston de Sonis, was born in Philadelphia, on No. 3 South Street, where the family had taken refuge because of the French Revolution. He was an officer in the French Army and was stationed in the West Indies at the time of his son's birth. Marie Elisabeth de Bébian had by a first marriage a daughter named Aline before Louis-Gaston arrived two years later. Two more children followed: Marie, who was called in childhood "Eglantine," born in 1828, and a brother Théobald, born in 1831.

For seven years the little Gaston grew up in the enchanting atmosphere of the Antilles, whose exotic perfumes and tropical verdure left an ineffaceable mark on his young mind. One nocturnal boat ride in particular was never to be forgotten. "I was lying in the bottom of the piroque rowed by some dozen Negroes, my head turned towards the sky, brilliant with stars. The silence of the night was broken only by the rhythmic plunges of the oars. God revealed Himself for the first time to my soul; my heart

The next morning Gaston awoke to find a friend of his father's in his room, the bearer of the cruelest of news: Major de Sonis had had a hemorrhage and was dying in a hotel at Bordeaux. A carriage was sent and the children departed at once. They found their father lying in his agony, unable to speak a word. In the next room, the song and dance of a hotel party contrasted strangely with their sobs.

"Night came," wrote Gaston. "I saw a priest enter and I threw myself in front of him to prevent his entrance, through what human prudence I know not, but in the fear that the sight of a priest would make my father realize the gravity of his state. Fortunately, my sisters drew me out of the room and let the priest pass so that he could fulfill the duties of his ministry. When he had heard my father's confession, my sisters fetched me and we entered the room all together. My father was calm. He asked for his watch and gold chain and put them in my hand as a parting souvenir."

A few hours later Major Charles-Gaston de Sonis peacefully breathed his last. It was midnight and the laughter of the party continued. "My sisters knelt at the foot of the bed where lay all that was left to us of what we had loved in this world. I sat by his head, holding one of his hands in mine. Thus the night passed. O my God! You know what I suffered. . . !" Early in the morning the door opened slowly and a priest entered. He was unknown to the children but someone had informed him of the tragedy in that hotel room. Praying first before the lifeless body, he said: "My children, I have just learned that you are in great sorrow. I am the minister of Jesus Christ. I am come to you to share your affliction and to bring you His consolations, if you so wish." He spoke for a long time, every word falling like dew on parched ground. Gaston listened attentively and opened his soul "eager for those holy words to which I had become unaccustomed for several years. When he left us, I was *converted*. Jesus Christ took possession again of my heart." This is what General de Sonis called his "conversion." The priest was Father Poncet, the Jesuit. We shall see the black-robed sons of Spain's glorious soldier-saint helping the great soldier of France all along his march towards God.

The next morning the body of Major de Sonis was taken to Libourne. Gaston was broken with sorrow and too ill to be present in the cemetery but he heard the salute fired over his father's grave.

Major de Sonis left his son his coolheadedness and daring in battle and the love for the "noble profession of arms." Gaston inherited from his mother the inclination to prayer and the taste for the poetic and the beautiful. Both parents gave him his heart with its depths for love and boundless capacity for sacrifice, which seem to mark the French.

CHAPTER II

"Till Death Do Us Part"

Shortly after his father's death, Gaston departed for Saint-Cyr and his sisters returned to the Antilles. Théobald was at la Flèche. While Gaston's religion grew stronger in the daily struggles against the spirit of irreligion which prevailed in the military schools at that time, that of his brother was causing anxiety.

After two years as a brilliant student at Saint-Cyr, Gaston chose the cavalry and entered the famous training school at Saumur in 1846. The incident that seems to have made the deepest impression on him while at Saumur was a pilgrimage to the world famous Benedictine Abbey of Solesmes. When asked why he did not remain, he answered: "Because I do not have in me the stuff that makes a Benedictine." He retained from this visit a lifelong love for the liturgy and a certain nostalgia for the monastic life. With calm, he considered the dangers of the life ahead of him and promised his Divine Master "that aided by His grace, *I would refuse Him nothing*. One must not bargain with God." He kept his promise.

In April, 1848, he left Saumur as second lieutenant to the 5th Hussars. He was the most outstanding of the young officers. That summer he went with his regiment to the

15

city of Castres. An officer of the regiment which Gaston's was replacing spoke with highest praise of a young girl whose father was a lawyer of Castres. Who should appear at a window at that very moment but the subject of their conversation. The young girl looked down as de Sonis, a dashing officer in his brilliant hussar uniform, rode by. Their eyes met and their hearts were knit for life. On April 18, 1849, in the ancient Cathedral of St. Benedict, Louis-Gaston de Sonis and Antoinette-Anaïs Roger were united in wedlock. He was 23 and she only 17. Gaston could have made a brilliant marriage that would have freed him from all financial anxieties. He did not build his castles of glamor and vanity. Instead, he laid up his treasures in Heaven where the thief of materialism cannot break through nor the rust and moth of worldly pleasures destroy. He had a pearl of great price in his young wife and he lost nothing in Eternity by giving up all he could have had in this life to possess the hidden treasure she proved to be.

Free Masonry had gained influence under the government of that time, and being represented as a philanthropic society that respected religion, Gaston's companions persuaded him to join while he was a cadet at Saumur. He was unaware of the Church's condemnations. He had never been at a lodge, but one night shortly after his marriage, he attended a masonic dinner. He smiled at the strange decorations and costumes but then the speeches began. His surprise increased as he listened to one, then another. When Catholicism and priests were attacked, that ended his silence. "Oh, so this is a snare! I was told religion would always be respected, and it is insulted! You have not kept your promises, I am freed of mine. You will not see me again. Good-night!" Throwing down his napkin, he left abruptly the stupefied and irate diners.

The young couple were exemplary in every way. Their

16

happiness in each other consoled them for everything . . . "happiness as complete as can be dreamed of in this world," wrote Anaïs. "Every day we thanked God for giving us to each other. We really had but one heart and one soul. My Gaston's was a treasure of goodness and tenderness, a heart of exquisite sensitiveness and at the same time so virile and of rare firmness." Both of them were artists and they enjoyed spending their free time visiting works of art or indulging their brushes in their own creations. They also read together spiritual and philosophical works. Gaston had a passion for his profession and would revel in reading histories of battles and the art of military tactics. It was touching to see little Anaïs take up a tome and bury herself in the same literary matter to be like her husband. She even acquired a taste for such reading. She was the perfect companion. What is less remarkable, she also acquired a love and an efficiency for horseback riding so that she need not be separated from her beloved Gaston while he indulged in his lifelong favorite pastime. His passion for the horse was the means God was to use to set him on his way to sanctification.

De Sonis' regiment was sent to Brittany, then to Paris. These changes punctuate his entire military career to the end, and to the end his heroic wife will follow to the utmost of her power. At the beginning of each new move an almost daily correspondence followed, but the separation would prove intolerable and the young wife, accompanied by her father, would soon find herself installed in very modest lodgings, but she had him with whom alone she could be happy. In February, 1850, their first child was born at Castres, a little girl whom they named Marie.

The year 1850 saw Gaston a lieutenant. He was at Paris where he and his wife attended the inspiring sermons given by the great Dominican preacher, Father Lacordaire, at the Cathedral of Notre Dame. "I left there transported, fully penetrated with love for God and for the Church," Gaston wrote. While at Paris he had the happiness of being again with his sisters who were finishing their education. Shortly afterwards, Aline married Dr. Flandrin but she was to die young. Josephine entered the Carmel of Poitiers where she was soon appreciated for her gifted nature and mature qualities of heart and mind. Marie, the gay, beautiful "Eglantine" so fond of the world where she was a favorite, heard the Master's call and after hard struggles followed her sister to the Carmelite monastery. Gaston felt these partings keenly but he gave his sisters to God with full generosity.

The next move was to Limoges which was to be the scene of the springtime and the winter of de Sonis' military career. He entered it now a handsome lieutenant with a brilliant future. He was a young father of two children, for little Gaston had arrived to join the family hearth.

It was at Limoges that he found his boyhood friend of Juilly days—Henri Lamy de la Chapelle, like himself recently married. The two young wives soon became fast friends thus deepening the friendship of their husbands. One day when they were congratulating each other for the good taste of a cloth one of them had bought, Gaston was asked to fetch it, which he did willingly enough. Returning with the wonderful article, he daintily held it up, saying with his fine smile: "Ladies! *sic transit gloria mundi!*" (Thus passes the glory of the world.) There was something of the monk as well as of the knight in this young man.

Henri Lamy hastened to have his friend join the recently founded Conference of St. Vincent de Paul. Gaston was an indefatigable member. He soon endeared himself to the poor who called his visits "the sitting visit" because he would sit down beside them, take their hand in his and listen to all their troubles. Poor himself, he never was without a way of helping those less fortunate. The Archives of the Conference at Limoges show the extraordinary activity of this young lieutenant. He was seen in his colorful uniform going about the streets in an army wagon collecting clothes and other articles to be distributed by the Conference. If the Church raises him to the honors of her altars, perhaps Gaston de Sonis will be named patron of those engaged in Catholic Action. He would be a perfect model. His conduct could have aroused antagonism, but he was so gay and amiable, so natural in his goodness, so attentive to his military duties, that he was loved and admired by his companions, of whom, however he wrote: "I pity them with all my heart, for these poor officers know nothing but to drink, eat, sleep, and smoke. They find me very strange, I suppose, and no doubt brand me 'Jesuit' which is the general title given to those who love God and think a little about Him."

Gaston had a highly spirited English thoroughbred which he named Miss Anna. Almost every day he took her to the hippodrome outside the city where he was training her for the horseshow. One day in May, 1852, something startled the nervous creature and Miss Anna bounded sideways throwing her rider. For a long time Gaston lay unconscious. As soon as he recovered his senses, he insisted on being put in the saddle. Doubled over, he rode back to army quarters, a journey that seemed eternal. He again lost consciousness. He was carried to his home on a stretcher, like one dead. As soon as he could speak, he asked for a priest and prepared for death. For a month Gaston endured agonies of pain in his body, but his soul was to soar and never again to descend to earth. It was during this long retreat, which reminds one of the Saint of Loyola, that he realized "the nothingness of this world." He was

19

nursed back to life by Anaïs' devoted care, while God ploughed and seeded his soul. He guarded with silence this secret working of the Holy Spirit, which in spite of himself, became apparent, even exteriorly. Thenceforth, he went by gallops along the way of perfection.

Even before this accident, Gaston de Sonis had been an exemplary Christian. He had been attending Mass at the Cathedral at five in the morning no matter how severe the cold. From that time on the Blessed Sacrament became the center of his life. He made his meditation every day, received Holy Communion every week, which was rare in those days, and would stop in the church every afternoon to pay a visit to his Master or to make the Way of the Cross. In 1853, on Shrove Tuesday, he founded a nocturnal adoration group in the chapel of the Oblates of Mary Immaculate. He wrote about it to Louis de Sèze: "We thus tried to put in the scales of Divine judgment a little love on the side of mercy, which so often is lacking in our acts of atonement, so as to counterbalance the malice of men. We are eight Christians, a little like conspirators. We spend delightful nights. I have written to my Carmelite sisters so they can unite with us."

In May, 1854, Gaston was promoted to the rank of Captain to the 7th Hussars. This necessitated his departure for Algeria. All his life he was to regret Limoges, his second home, where he had many friends and happy memories. The keenest separation was from his wife who was expecting her fourth child; she had given birth to a second son, Henri, the year preceding. Since their marriage they had never been apart for more than three or four days at a time.

After tearing himself from her arms and the embraces of his children, de Sonis set out for Montpellier. From there he wrote to Henri Lamy de la Chapelle: "When I come back to my hotel room in midst of my baggage, I fall

20

into an arm chair like one stupefied, and the tears come to my eyes. I am incapable of doing anything. I can only think of the happiness I left behind. If you have something to suffer, my dear friend, think of me.

"I have a lot of plans concerning Africa. If I did not have vexations and I could take my wife, I would be very glad to go there. I think that I would be happy and that I would find much to study there. I may try to establish myself in Africa to remain for the rest of my days.

"I have no dreams about the rest. I consider that life is a very short time. For long I have been persuaded that it is nothing but what the Church defines it—a valley of tears. As I have told you, I have found there many thorns. I have also found some flowers and most beautiful ones, because I do not know if there is anything in this world superior to my dear Anaïs and you. So I often think of the end of life; I sigh for death as a traveler for repose. And if it were not for the sorrow of leaving someone behind us, and also the thought that each moment spent in this world can unite us closer to Jesus Christ, I would quickly say: 'My God, take me!'

"Adieu, my dear Henri, I send you what I have, my heart."

Gaston had one more sacrifice to make. He had hoped to take Miss Anna with him, but the authorities were unwilling to permit the transport of horses into Africa.

From Marseilles he wrote a last letter:

"I obtained several hours to go to Notre Dame de la Garde to pray . . . This sanctuary has produced an altogether divine effect on me . . . In leaving this soil of France I cannot hold back some tears which are the last heritage that I bequeath to all that I love in this world. Adieu, my dear Henri . . . Pray for me . . ."

From Algerian shores he wrote: "Long and interesting

conversations from which I was unable to tear myself away until I had said three or four times that I had to leave. They are precious souvenirs for one who has nothing left of life, alas, but souvenirs."

Yes, Anaïs was right. The heart of her Gaston "was a treasure of goodness and tenderness and of exquisite sensitiveness."

CHAPTER III

Africa

Today Africa is occupying world attention. A hundred years ago it was a land in some respects much as it is today; in others, vastly different. Since 1830 France was pushing her authority farther and farther. Marshal Bugeaud was sent there with the mission to pacify and colonize it. In six and a half years he defeated Abd-el-Kader, the Emir, broke the strength of Morocco by the victory of Isly, pushed the occupation to Laghouat on the border of the Sahara, opened roads, founded villages and attracted colonists who furthered agricultural progress. The changing governments at home interfered with this colonization, and the Crimean War took the best of the French troops. Tribes revolted and retreated into their impregnable natural fortresses of the Kabylia and Djurjura regions, thereby threatening the work so well begun. The bugle called the soldier to action at any moment as insurrections flared up first from one quarter, then from another. There is no fiercer warrior than the Arab who marches to a "holy war." But it is not the Africa of a hundred years ago that concerns us here, nor the Africa of today. Nor is it even the battles and exploits, fascinating as they can be, of our young hero that concern us. Keeping strictly to the purpose of this book and to the promise not to detain you long, we shall confine ourselves to the study of the hero himself, to see how he accepted the circumstances of his life and used them for his sanctification on his march to God.

Captain de Sonis set up his headquarters at Mustapha on the heights of Algiers. He was in command of a squadron of Hussars. The country appealed to this "child of the islands," as he liked to call himself. He thus described to Louis de Sèze his modest installation: two rooms, an iron bed, a few chairs, some books—his "faithful friends." "But what would not make me change my cabin for a castle is the magnificent panorama seen from my windows. You cannot imagine anything more beautiful. To my left I have Algiers, before me the beach and camp of Mustapha, and on the right, the mountains of Kabylia and Atlas. Finally, all this is bordered by a limitless sea always covered with ships.

"What moments I spend at my window! I like to dream and meditate above all at night. . . . How small I see myself in presence of this gigantic nature! I have never felt my nothingness more, but also I have never hoped more in the infinite mercy of this God Who made us so little only to incite us to elevate ourselves to Him and Who extends His hand to us."

If the natural beauty of the country helped his meditations, the immorality and over-gay life of the soldiers and colonists nauseated him, and the little place given to God sickened his soul. In strange contrast to this was the native population "eminently religious and so attached to the errors of Islamism that it is painful to think what little hope there is of christianizing it. Fortunately, the ways of Providence are unknown to us and we can hope an hour will come when these unhappy people will open their eyes to the light."

It was the same in Africa as in France: Gaston took an open stand and made no secret of his religious beliefs. "That is essential," he wrote, "because that done, God takes charge of the rest, and He rewards generously the little one does for Him." He won the respect of his companions by his attitude at once firm, open and courageous. A veneration surrounded him. The soldiers died like flies when the cholera passed over the camp. Then it was they saw their Captain at his true worth, and they lost their hearts to him. He was prodigious in his charity, caring for the afflicted and oblivious of his own safety.

It was not the cholera that tracked down de Sonis but burning fevers. These brought him to the brink of the grave. As he lay in his poor hut thinking of his adored wife and young children who were depending on him for support, he begged God to remove the chalice pressed to his lips. He laid everything at the foot of the Cross and pronounced his *fiat*. This time the chalice was withdrawn.

The seed planted during the long retreat at Limoges, after the accident with Miss Anna, continued to grow. It was planted in good ground capable of yielding a hundredfold, so it had to be cultivated accordingly. For five years the mettle of his soul was forged in the heat of desolation, his character chiseled by the intense trials interior and exterior that God uses to shape and sanctify His saints. Like his Divine Master, the servant came forth in the power of the Spirit. A mortal sadness clutched his soul as the solitude bore down mercilessly on his sensitive heart. How could he live so far from those he loved? Anaïs' soft caresses were not there to cool the scorching fever; the silence seemed intolerable as childish laughter and patter of little feet echoed only in memory. There are soldiers today going through the same sufferings, far from home and all they love, and living with those with whom they cannot share their thoughts and aspirations. Anyone who knows the agony of loneliness, which St. John of the Cross likens to a file, can find an understanding friend and support in Gaston de Sonis.

Let us see now how our hero mastered his trial: "I find myself very alone here, surrounded by people I practically do not know, and who share none of my thoughts. . . . As soon as my service is done, and the meals which we take in common finished, I ride my horse back to my dwelling. There I take up some book and my day thus passes between study and some good moments of meditation. At first it was painful to adapt myself to this existence. I love my wife and children so much that it seemed I could not make myself live so far from them, but I put all this at the foot of the Cross. . . . I even like to think that I shall have something to gain from this new state in which Divine Providence has put me. I often recall these words of Scripture: 'I will lead her into solitude, and there I will speak to her heart.' May my heart be worthy, or rather be not too unworthy, to listen to this voice!"

Here is where too many of us part from our hero. We try to escape from suffering, to deafen the interior voice. Our Lady said at Fatima that the sacrifices She was asking were the acceptance of the daily trials Her Son sends us. We are avid to discover and try new pain-killers, new short cuts to make life easier by eliminating the labor of living. Machines do our thinking for us, while noise and rush drown the possibility of concentrating. Glamor, sensation, headlines, living on the surface of life—that is it! What have we to do with you, Miles Christi?

Earlier in this chapter we saw some books in Gaston's humble dwelling. Among these "faithful friends" were the Bible, the Holy Gospel in Arabic, some Arabian works, the *Imitation of Christ* in Latin, St. Augustine, the great saint of Africa, and Virgil—"in remembrance of the poetry and arts I loved so much." On the first page of the *Imitation,* he would have read these words: "Let it be our chief study to meditate on the life of Jesus Christ. . . . He who would fully and feelingly understand the words of Christ must study to make his whole life conformable to that of Christ." This is just what de Sonis did with his life. When he left his anguish "at the foot of the Cross," he abandoned himself to Him Who hung upon it, and while meditating on his Master's sufferings, his own grew light.

To satisfy an increasing desire to be alone with the Alone, He made a closed retreat at the Trappist monastery of Staouëli under the direction of its Abbot—Father Francis Regis. This man of God had founded the monastery twelve years before. Walking over insuperable difficulties and the graves of thirty of his monks, he founded his monastery on the very field of the battle of Staouëli. It is a flourishing oasis in a desert witnessing to the grace of God and the persevering effort of indomitable courage. Gaston left this retreat transfigured. He wished all the officers to pass through that school of Christ. One thinks spontaneously of the rich harvest the Trappists in our own country reaped after World War II. Is not the Trappist a Miles Christi ever on duty?

De Sonis' answer to the Master's call to an ever closer union was to establish a nocturnal adoration society at

27

Algiers as he had done at Limoges. Gathering a group of elite Christians, they spent the entire night once a month before the God of mercy in the Blessed Sacrament, so outraged and blasphemed in that vast country. The reunions took place, he wrote, "in the chapel of the Jesuit Fathers who are here, as everywhere, at the head of all good works." It is wonderful to think that such an act of faith and love was established on African soil and by a young officer of the French Army!

What was the Master's answer to His servant? He took the heart of that servant and made of it an altar of pure holocaust. God knows what is in man, and here was one capable of wrestling with God. His letters at this period were written with his blood. His trials were terrific. To de Sèze: "Pray for me, my dear Louis, I have need of it. I have great need of strength to endure what I cannot tell you in a letter. Life is so made that when one wound is healed another opens more piercing than the first. . . . You will think of me when you will be at the foot of that Cross which we learned together to love, when life was open to our dreams and illusions. . . ! I do not complain, because God is so good that He never strikes me but to make me better. And besides, has He not given me what should console me in all my pains: the affection of my dear wife, who is certainly one of the best persons in this world."

These lines from St. John of the Cross' "Living Flame of Love," Stanza II, will flash a light on the sufferings he could not relate in a letter. "This is the way God deals with those whom it is His will to exalt. He suffers them to be tempted, afflicted, tormented and chastened, inwardly and outwardly, to the utmost limit of their strength, that He may deify them, unite them to Himself in His wisdom which is the highest state, purifying them . . . the words

28

of Our Lord are chaste words, silver, examined by fire, tested in the earth of our flesh and purified seven times, that is, made perfectly pure.

"But it is very necessary for the soul to endure these tribulations and trials, inward and outward, spiritual and corporal, great and small, with great resolution and patience, accepting all as from the hand of God for its healing and its good, not shrinking from them, because they are for the health of the soul. . . . We are, therefore, to count it a great favor when Our Lord sends us interior and exterior trials, remembering that they are few in number who deserve to be made perfect through sufferings so as to attain to so high a state as this."

There is no artificer so skillful as the Divine Artist, nor is the creation of the universe so great and delicate a work as the fashioning of man to sanctity. God thrusts the soul into the heat of His love and removes it from time to time to view the progress in the mirroring of His Christ. Our hero was no exception; he too had his moments of respite. Anaïs had given him a fourth child, Albert, and was able to join him with the eldest children, Marie and Gaston. Their installation was at Milianah near the desert where the gazelles frolicked. There were happy hours spent together, often on horseback visiting Arab chiefs and following hunting expeditions. The children gamboled about the inner court among the palm and orange trees. They were old enough to have the catechism explained to them—a duty their father proudly took upon himself.

These assignments were never of long duration. By the end of his life, Sonis had changed garrisons over twenty times. These changes were made at his own expense, which was ruinous to his already thin purse. From Milianah he was called to Blidah, and from there back to Algiers, where he took up quarters again at Mustapha. In August, 1856, the 7th Hussars were called to the Djurjura to put down a revolt. Madame de Sonis had to return to France with the two children. "My finances were so exhausted by the unbelievable expense caused by my continual changes and the excessive price of everything in this country," Gaston wrote, "that I was forced to separate from what is my only consolation in this world. I had great difficulty in coming to this decision and in drying the tears of my poor wife, and I think my heart would have failed me, if we both had not asked courage of Him Who is the source. ... It was very hard! But God of Whom I asked resignation gave me a little and I could, besides, thank Him, because apart from the trials that my financial difficulties cause me, I do not know if there is interior happiness more perfect than mine."

In October the expedition into the South was successfully terminated, and Gaston obtained leave to join his family at Castres. He dreamed of a peaceful life in the country surrounded by his family and friends in which he could devote himself to his children's education. But the Divine Master had other plans for him. "What happiness to fashion together these young souls for Heaven, and to prepare for the battles of the world these tender hearts! I never think of that without emotion, because I can own in all conscience that I have never known worldly ambition, and that I have no dreams but that. But God has not willed it; let us submit to His holy Will. To be a Christian is just that ... Love and resignation. There is the whole of Christianity."

The following January, 1857, Madame de Sonis gave birth to their fifth child, a little girl whom they named Marie-Thérèse. She was destined to die in childhood.

In the spring, Marshal Randon, who was governor at Algiers, prepared an expedition against the Kabylia that was to be decisive. Gaston had to separate again from his family.

In May the French troops attained the summits of the mountains, after superhuman labor, and received at Souk-el-Arbâ the submission of the Ben-Raten, the most powerful of the Kabylian tribes. A Mass of thanksgiving was celebrated in open air by the vicar general of Algiers. He took for his sermon the words inscribed on a stone that the French soldiers had come across high up on the mountains and which dated from Roman times: "O Christ! may You hold firmly with Your followers this country before our eyes!" We know our young Captain well enough by now to be able to imagine how deeply each word must have inscribed itself in his heart.

In 18 days a road 25 kilometers (about 12 miles) long and 6 meters wide was laid through impenetrable crags. As Fort-National rose, the Kabylian tribes understood that the tomb of their independence was built. During the whole expedition de Sonis showed himself to be a soldier without fear and a Christian without reproach.

In September he was sent to Blidah, his "sixth garrison in 18 months," then in February to Orléansville. Suddenly the 7th Hussars were recalled to France. Because he could expect to rise to the grade of major sooner, he asked to be changed to the 1st *Chasseurs d'Afrique,* who were stationed at Algiers and who did not go out except for campaigns. The *Chasseurs d'Afrique* are elite troops of light cavalry given especially hard training. Once again de Sonis renounced the sweet dream of being with his family for the sake of supporting this family, which now counted 6 children, for Madeleine was born during this year. Colonel de Salignac-Fénelon and the officers of the 1st *Chasseurs* received him with joy. One of them describes Miles Christi thus: "The hero was still young, tall, of slight build, a very skillful rider, well-informed, modest, very affable and friendly towards everyone but very severe towards himself and a strict observer of discipline. He very soon won us all." This was in March 1858. Our Lady Immaculate was appearing beyond the Pyrennes to Bernadette of Lourdes. The Virgin Mother was to become in a singular way the mother of Miles Christi.

Understanding the situation between Moslem and Christian better than those in high places, Gaston de Sonis set himself to the task of learning the Arabian language. He mastered it so well that no officer of his time knew it better, if as well. He could speak fluently and write, not only classic Arabic, but also the popular Arab dialects used by many of the common people. This could have given him an advantageous position at an Arabian office or as instructor of the troops at Tunis. These positions were obtained through influence, to which Miles Christi would not bow. He felt himself sufficiently burdened without adding the debt of having to repay a favor. His promotion in the army was won by the valor of his sword alone. Louis de Sèze took it upon himself to interest an influential person in his friend. Sonis reproached him when he heard of it. His letter ends: "I believe that if sometimes it can become a duty to ask an alms, if it is permitted a Christian to beg his bread, when he and his children have none, it is not written anywhere that he must *beg for favors.*"

His sufferings made him more tender toward others. His aim was to make his religion attractive to all by rendering every kind of little service. Marie de Sonis recorded this incident of her childhood. She was playing in the vestibule of the officers' quarters when she saw a soldier in tears enter and fall at her father's knees. "Captain, my mother, my poor mother is dead." Her father put his arms around the young man and took him to his own room. There he consoled him with words and tenderness for a long time until the young soldier was comforted and resigned to his cross.

If any of his companions was ill, he would hasten to his bedside, and suggesting holy thoughts, would prepare him to receive the priest. The Pastor at Mustapha wrote about him: "Constant prayer and frequent Communion raised him daily nearer and nearer perfection. Whenever my ministry brought me into closer contact with this soul, I felt inspired to greater zeal and devotion in my duties as priest and minister."

His sensitiveness to the sufferings of others and the quality of his friendship are seen in a magnificent letter of condolence to Henri Lamy, who had lost his father-in-law. To quote in part: "I feel that my pen is powerless to dry your tears, but I am very sure that my heart is not. From the bottom of our hearts, we have asked God to finish the work of his mercy. We have asked it often and we will ask it again. May this be the gauge and bond of our affection . . . Your sorrow is only of this world and this world is so little a thing . . . ! I ask you to unite yourself to us on the day of the Resurrection of the Saviour and to receive the Holy Eucharist, penetrated with the thought that He Who has triumphed over death has also caused him to triumph for whom you weep.

"Next month I depart with all my regiment for an expedition to the South. I shall be absent about a month. My poor wife will remain here alone with the children. I need not tell you we are very sad . . . Adieu, dear Henri

... Anaïs and I wish to tell you again that the remembrance of you is always with us. In losing you, we have lost all that one can love. Pray a little for us. Your best friend, G. DE SONIS."

He returned from the South broken with fevers when an unexpected order called him to a new battlefield, but he had one last joy before leaving Mustapha. Encouraged by his colonel and the pastor, de Sonis took the initiative in having a large iron cross erected at the turn of the road frequented by officer and soldier. The whole parish assisted; the bishop blessed it and all the officers were present, while the military band played. Far from disapproving, the Moslems applauded this bold act of faith. De Sonis always felt "that Algeria would never be conquered by France until the Christian religion was firmly established; and that more would be done by the cross than by the sword."

CHAPTER IV

The New Battlefield

~~~~~~

Napolean III dragged France into war against Austria by promising Cavour, the statesman, to help Italy free the Lombard-Venetian states. He himself led an army of over a hundred thousand men. The 1st *Chasseurs d'Afrique* formed part of it. Catholics all over the world were alarmed. From the beginning, Sonis looked on the whole affair with distrust, considering the campaign inauspicious for France, the Church, and Italy. He was given the order to fight, so he prepared himself for combat. He was a soldier; he knew his duty, so he sacrificed his own judgments.

On May 17, 1859, after a miserable crossing in an old ship, Captain de Sonis disembarked at Genoa with his regiment. The French soldiers were all but smothered under the shower of flowers and Italian embraces that accompanied the loud shouts of "eternal thanks to the liberators of Italy." There were triumphant entrances into the cities, but, from the start, de Sonis looked upon these demonstrations with silent misgivings.

While other officers had to receive an order to moderate the way they set up tent at each stop, Gaston described his dwelling to Father Brumauld, of the Company of Jesus,

35

his friend in Africa: "I do not know whether you can read what I am writing, for it is an awful scribble. I am writing under difficulty, however, for my only house, or rather den, is two knapsacks propped against two rifles, and it is under this too thin roof that we receive the deluges of rain that water us every day. Moreover, I truly love my little roof of canvas. It is a great happiness to be able to taste here a little evangelical poverty." He wrote to his Carmelite sister at Poitiers: "I had to lighten my baggage so much that I brought with me only *The Imitation of Christ* that you gave me. This book is always in my hands; but I had a veritable need of nourishing myself with Holy Scriptures. A friend lent me his *New Testament,* but besides depriving him of it, I have difficulty getting it sometimes. Send me a copy if it does not cost too much."

The Holy Scriptures and *The Imitation of Christ* were the two inexhaustible mines that served de Sonis for his prayer during his whole life. All his efforts were bent on putting into practice what he learned from those pure sources. He gave all his spare time to visiting the wounded of both armies in the improvised hospitals. The humblest heart could experience a thrill of national pride at the heroism with which the soldiers were enduring their sufferings. Those who might lose a member when the doctor reached their side smiled bravely when an illustrious marshal passed among them. Showing them his stump of an arm, he said: "Courage, my boys, I have passed that way!"

There was another soldier, less illustrious, who would pass along those heaps of human suffering. Sonis had a way all his own of encouraging and consoling. As soon as his service was over, he would spend his time helping to transport the fallen in battle and dressing their wounds.

He praised their courage as soldiers and lifted their minds to the supreme Master, the Divine Leader, Who Himself "has passed that way." He would compliment them on their military conduct and then in his simple, direct and ardent way propose Jesus Christ as their Model and Friend, suggest a few short aspirations that a man in pain could repeat without too much fatigue. Before leaving him, the sufferer had to have a blest medal. When the priest followed where Sonis had passed, he found hearts open and ready, because those strong men saw Jesus of Nazareth passing by in the passing of the Soldier of Christ, Miles Christi.

Out on reconnaissance, Sonis would search for a steeple, and shortly after sighting it, would be kneeling at the feet of an old priest to make his confession. He did not know Italian nor the priest French, but he made himself understood in his Latin of school days. He would receive his Eucharistic Master and then make his thanksgiving on the gallop, "joyous of heart, ready for all sacrifice . . . What a delightful Companion Our Lord is. The disciples of Emmaus were quite right!" Despite his silence and modesty, his comrades were not long in finding out where he spent the time that others gave to well-deserved rest. Veneration soon surrounded him. He was prodigious in accomplishing his military duties, giving his men an example of activity and discipline, preparing them for combat and impatient for his turn. "In all this he was obeying his conscience," recounts a lieutenant who made the campaign at his side, "because although he never said a word about it, I was not slow to notice that this Italian war did not please him at all." There is much in common in the training of a soldier and the making of a monk.

In the middle of the night of June 24th, de Sonis'

regiment received the order to prepare to attack. Wasted with fever—for two days Gaston had taken nothing—he refused to be relieved and remained at his post. The 1st *Chasseurs* left the camp at 3 a.m. and by morning reached the plain of Solferino, where the French and Austrian troops met. A bullet passed between the legs of Gaston's horse, killing the one behind him. "Death seemed imminent, but I had made the sacrifice of my life, and I thought that if God judged me necessary to my family, He would preserve me from all evil." Towards evening Marshal Niel's corps weakened and the French munitions began to run low. The Austrians perceiving this, thrust their infantry on Niel. We shall let Captain de Sonis tell the story.

"While we were exhausting our ammunition, the Austrian infantry was pouncing upon Niel. The general commanding our division received the order for us to attack. Our two squadrons were superb and our support was impatiently awaited by the infantry. Niel's corps was succumbing to superior numbers. The general called to the 1st *Chasseurs d'Afrique* forming the front line to lead the attack but his voice was lost in the din and no one heard him. The situation was too urgent for further delay, so General Desvaux turned to my squadron. I heard his call and trotted up to him. With a voice full of feeling, for he realized he was sacrificing us, he told me to close in under rifle fire but not to make the final assault until he had ordered both wings to attack with us. I pointed out to the general that we would all be picked off one by one by the powerful enemy forces lying under cover of the woods before our rifle fire could be of any effect. I asked his permission to charge without further delay.

He thought it over quickly and replied, 'Yes, you are right! Charge without further delay, right now!'

"I turned back to my squadron, gave the order to charge, and dashed forward myself at full gallop. I felt no qualms and had peace of heart such as is known only in instances of great inner tranquility. My faith was complete. Leading my men by several yards, I made a fine target.

"We reached the edge of the woods at a sweeping gallop. The enemy infantry fell back at our approach but I tried to cut through them so as to roll them back against our lines. When we got into the middle of the woods, however, we encountered a withering rolling fire from every direction. I saw Tyrolian troops drawn up into exemplary squares. I tried to rally enough cavalrymen to break through a square, but my men fell on every side of me. In a burst of fury, I charged the squares myself and suddenly saw in front of my eyes a sea of faces I shall never forget. Bayonets flashed and my ears rang with countless shots. I found myself completely separated from my men. Part of my squadron was lying on the ground and the rest was fighting off a flanking attack by a squadron of hussars. My poor grey charger received a mortal wound, but when I put the spurs to him he gathered enough remaining strength to get me out of the tangle before dropping dead twenty paces further. I jumped out of the saddle, parried a death-dealing bayonet thrust with my sabre and got away under a hail of bullets.

"I had therefore to run on foot towards our lines, sabre in hand. One of my chasseurs brought me a horse." This chasseur, Decroix by name, wanted to give his captain his own horse, but Sonis refused, saying: "Your life is worth mine." Decroix then brought a horse that no longer had a rider. To finish, in Gaston's words:

"I mounted it and rallied my men . . .

"I had started the day with a magnificent squadron and when it was over all I had left was the complement of a platoon. But our action had saved Niel's corps from destruction and we had maintained a great tradition. When the battle was over, we had to water our horses ten miles away. We did not get back to our bivouac until two o'clock in the morning after twenty-four hours in the saddle without food or drink."

The fever that before consumed him disappeared during the battle. Before giving the command to charge—passing his sabre to his left hand with lightning speed—he made a large sign of the cross. He was able to write to his Carmelite sister: "I believe I did not lose sight of the presence of God for a single instant during the whole of that terrible day." Such interior recollection is the fruit of long and arduous effort.

A terrific thunderstorm which drowned even the roar of the cannon put an end to the battle. Seventeen thousand French soldiers and twenty-four thousand Austrians strewed the plain in death.

"On the morrow we buried our comrades. I shall never forget that scene. All were laid in the same trench, clothed in their uniforms as for battle. An Italian priest blest this vast tomb." Sonis visited his wounded men in the stable that served for hospital. Stretched out on straw, they waited for the surgeons who had to cut and saw like butchers . . . if death did not reach them first. "Those most to be pitied are those who cannot be picked up and who pass the night on the battlefield." Did he remember, one December night, that he had penned these words eleven years before? At least now it was the warm air of an Italian summer that hushed the battlefield this June night.

Solferino, June 24, 1859, was the decisive battle of the Italian-Austrian Campaign. Captain de Sonis had shown more than valor—he was a brilliant tactician. He was decorated with the Legion of Honor for his magnificent conduct. "May God bless all those who have prayed for my preservation," he wrote. "May He pardon me if I have given the impression that I am anything but what I am, the weakest and most miserable of creatures. Pray that I may become what I ought to be."

He had the disappointment of having to remain on in Italy with the army of occupation when he could so legitimately have hoped to return to Castres on home leave, a disappointment fully shared by the waiting wife and children. "It is time I tasted some calm in the midst of my little tribe. May the will of God be done! We, Christians and soldiers, must be twice over men of duty. I have tried to prove it during the whole of this campaign."

His whole thought is expressed in these lines: "God miraculously preserved my life. May I use it for His service and glory! That is my whole ambition."

CHAPTER V

Africa Again

On August 22, 1859, Gaston left the fair land of Italy for Africa, which was to claim eleven years more of his life. It was the eve of his 34th birthday. A Moroccan prince, true or pretended, had stirred up some tribes by proclaiming "a holy war." French frontier posts had been attacked and soldiers had been killed.

An expeditionary force was organized and Sonis asked to be changed from the 3rd to the 1st squadron of the *Chasseurs d'Afrique* as it formed part of the expeditionary force. Why? The eternal question of supporting his family. He wanted his advancement due to his services alone. He also believed he could serve his God and his country better on campaign than in garrison.

The colonel in command of the 1st squadron was Arthur de Montalembert, younger and worthy brother of the famous orator and author. Like Sonis, he had left a young wife and five children. Like Sonis, he was ardent in his Catholic beliefs. They had much in common and were immediately drawn to each other.

After a march of fifteen days, the troops reached Oran. The rivers were dried up; the ground was like powder, for it had not rained for weeks. They crossed the River Kis that divided at that point Algeria from Morocco and bivouacked in enemy territory. Fifteen thousand men found themselves grouped under the commander-in-chief, General de Martimprey. An enemy, far more formidable than the Arab, entered the camp and death followed in his wake. "The cholera!" was whispered along the lines. A wave of panic passed over the soldiers. Victims fell by hundreds, infesting the morale with discouragement. In this hideous nightmare, de Sonis astonished everyone by his calm. "Only that will happen which God wills. Let us first do our duty. I leave the rest in the hands of God." He explained later how he was able to keep his soul in peace during that time of general consternation and discouragement.

"I had made the sacrifice of my life, although it cost me much because of my wife and children. But, after all, God is a father. I had confidence in Him. I had taken care to unite myself to Him from the departure, and living in His presence, I was preserved, I hope, in His grace. I put myself at His orders. I was heartbroken to see those soldiers whom I loved fall every day like flies, without anyone to help them think of God. We had no chaplains. I often heard Colonel de Montalembert deplore this loudly. He suffered from it as did I. I did what I could for those poor dying soldiers. I was well paid by consolations of every kind that I found in assisting them. . . .

"People do not know what hearts of gold are under that rough bark. As soon as they felt themselves stricken, they turned to God, and I saw some deaths such as I wish to die myself. Poor young fellows! They confided to me their last recommendations. Sometimes it was heart rending. They prayed, in spite of their atrocious sufferings. I gave them my Crucifix to kiss. I quite rightly counted on the Sacred Heart of Jesus Who helped me greatly." The testimony of a witness to this heroic charity may be interesting:

"From our arrival at the bivouac of Kis, we had a lugubrious spectacle before our eyes. . . . All who fell sick were doomed. We lacked everything: chaplains, medical corps, doctors, even clean water, because all was dried up. But Captain de Sonis found himself in his proper element, which was charity. As the epidemic progressed, his abnegation worked greater marvels. He scarcely left the hospital. The greater number of those unfortunate men will thank Heaven for the consolations they owe him. He multiplied himself so as not to leave them, day or night. After their death, those who remained saw him still there, to perform the last duties to those hideous remains that one could hardly find the means of burying.

"He never spoke of his services. Someone recounted at our table that a certain chasseur had died in the night. The Captain was visibly moved as by painful news. We learned afterwards that he himself had passed the night at the side of that man and that he had not left him until he had breathed his last."

The cholera had neither respect for persons nor mercy. The 1st *Chasseurs d'Afrique* had escaped contagion, due partly to the duty of reconnaissance which was assigned to that regiment. It was a relief to get away from the deadly atmosphere, but the return was inevitable. Meals were taken almost in silence. Every morning a slow procession filed out with the bodies of those who had died during the night. Colonel de Montalembert had military airs played to keep up the morale. The refrains were taken up, down to the last soldier. Consternation swept the brave regiment in the sacrifice demanded of its two head officers. Young

44

Lieutenant-Colonel Fenin, married only a few months, was struck down first. Handing his purse to Colonel de Montalembert, he asked him to deliver it to his wife with his last farewell. The bride of a few months received the parting souvenir from someone else. On leaving Fenin's tent, Colonel de Montalembert handed the purse to another officer with these words: 'It is you, not I, who will fulfill this sad mission. As for me, it is finished.' "

A few days later, Colonel Arthur de Montalembert died a death worthy of the son of the Crusaders that he was. Captain de Sonis was at his side, lifting his thoughts above all earthly things, as he had done for Lieutenant-Colonel Fenin. In both cases, as with many of the other dying soldiers, de Sonis was asked to hear their confession and transmit it to a priest when one could be obtained. He tried to defend himself as not qualified, but in charity he had to receive many such confidences. He would never speak of this charity afterwards even to his wife. He galloped to Oran and brought back a Jesuit, Father Mermillod. The pale and contorted faces of the agonizing lit with hope when the son of Spain's sainted-soldier entered the tents; His sacred ministry was rendered easy by Captain de Sonis having administered his charity first. Five or six chaplains had been assigned to accompany the expeditionary force, but by an unhappy concurrence of difficulties, only two could reach their post. God draws good out of evil, and in the lack of priest He raised up lay-priests, so to speak.

The Army reached the heights of Ain-Taforalt where the enemy retreated, and after little resistance the French were in command.

The cholera continued to decimate the troops until their return to Algiers. It was a dismal sight to see many a soldier leading a riderless horse. Death had exterminated one quarter of the expeditionary force. For his military valor, Captain de Sonis was promoted Major to the 2nd Spahis, to the general rejoicing of the Army. As to his indefatigable battle against the real enemy, the newspapers were silent, but the heroism of Miles Christi is written in the Book of Life.

From December 1859 to March 1860, Gaston was with his family in France. He visited his Carmelite sisters in their monastery at Poitiers. Josephine was now Sister Marie-Thérèse of Jesus; Marie, the gay "Eglantine", was given the name Marie of the Blessed Sacrament.

The Carmel of Poitiers was founded in 1630. In March 1838, two religious of the community and four novices left their venerable monastery to found the Carmel of Lisieux. One of the two professed religious was Sister Geneviève of Saint Teresa. Everyone who has read the *Autobiography of St. Thérèse of the Child Jesus* knows how much the Saint esteemed the holiness of the foundress of her monastery.

While at the Carmel of Poitiers, Gaston joined the Third Order of Carmel, receiving the habit from Monsignor Gay. He wrote to Henri Lamy de la Chapelle: "I prayed much for you at Holy Communion, which I had the happiness of receiving in the chapel of Carmel. It seemed to me, for many reasons, that there my prayer had two wings and ascended to Heaven better."

He wanted his children to profit by the guardianship of his sisters; he also did not want them to suffer from the nomadic life of their father. He placed his two eldest sons, Gaston and Henri, with the Jesuits at Poitiers, and Marie, his "first born," with the Religious of the Sacred Heart in that city. The happy days of vacation were drawing to a rapid close. He had spent them with his family, and visiting friends and holy places of his predilection, such as the Church of Saint Germaine Cousin at Pibrac.

No sooner had Major de Sonis reached his new post at Mascara than he was made commandant of the territory of Ténès. "I am quite happy in my new position," he wrote to Louis de Sèze. "I look on it as a promotion, because I can consider myself as absolute head of the region that I command and administer. . . . I am dependent only on my general. . . . My territory, which is larger than several Departments in France, is not very populated." Ténès was a little town of about 5,000 inhabitants, situated on the Mediterranean, west of Algiers. There were no French villages, only Arab encampments. "Ténès is a lovely little town in a picturesque position in the midst of a superb country," wrote de Sonis. "The climate is very healthful; sicknesses are rare,—an eminently important matter for a father of a family. I found here a good lodging for which I did not have to pay, furnished by the State, something greatly appreciated by me, as you can imagine. I have therefore every reason to believe that my wife will be happy here, and that is all I ask. I am overjoyed at thinking that perhaps I can pass a few happy years here, surrounded by my little family."

Gaston turned to God in joy as well as in trial. He wrote to his friend, Louis de Sèze: "The longer I live the more I attach myself with my whole heart to our holy religion that has so divinely supported me in my trials. I have not done much for God, but I have, at least, the will and the firm resolution of walking in the Christian way. So many conspire against our Divine Master and against His holy Church. Should we not attach ourselves to Him with love as strong as the hatred of which He is the object? This hatred must be the measure of our love. May this measure be able to satisfy the Heart of Jesus!"

Madame de Sonis and the younger children joined Gaston in May. The happy days of family life were overshadowed by the outbreak of war at Rome. The Papal States were invaded. What did this mean, to the Soldier of Christ, to the soldier and son of the first Daughter of the Church?

"I am more and more overwhelmed by what I read in the newspapers. . . . What blindness! What conspiracy against truth and common sense! If I were not responsible before God for the life, the education and future of my children, if my dear wife had not bound her lot with mine, how far I would be from here! With what joy would I not give my arm to the service of the Holy Father! And what death could be more worthy of envy than the one they will find in this holy war who have left family and country to help the only throne still worthy of sovereign majesty! It is the last refuge of truth on this earth given over more than ever to error and iniquity. But I must command silence to a heart that beats, alas, too loudly. Each one to his duty. It is only too true that God does not let us choose our cross."

The work Sonis wanted to do at Ténès was to give true civilization, which is the civilization of the Church, not only to the members of the Army and the settlers, but also to the Arabs subject to the French.

"I believe that there is some good to be done around me by reason of my position, and it is in this sense that I will try to accomplish the work of Providence, which uses the most unworthy instruments for arriving at its end."

The administration of tribes whose submission was only on the surface was an extremely difficult and delicate matter. Understanding the situation better than those in high places, Major de Sonis had set himself to the task of learning the Arabian language when he had first landed on African soil. This enabled him to enter into direct contact with the natives. It was a novel experience for them to have their governor arrive in their midst accompanied by his wife and escort. A married man, the father of a large family, could with ease enter their tent-homes, sit down among them and listen to all their troubles. They soon found out they could depend on him for strict justice. The poor Arab received as much attention and courtesy as the richest Moslem. What amazed them most was his disinterestedness; he could not be bribed or persuaded to accept presents. Major de Sonis was to raise his country's moral honor by the strict and disinterested administration of his justice.

In November, 1860, the military government at Algiers was re-established, with Marshal Pélissier as governor and General de Martimprey *chargé d'affaires.* Major de Sonis was sent as commandant of the territory of Lahgouat. At that time Laghouat was on the southern confines of the French conquests and was still a post of combats—therefore a post of honor and confidence, requiring of its governor both military skill and governing ability.

A hundred years ago Laghouat was an attractive oasis with a town of 3,000 or 4,000 inhabitants. It was watered by a small river issuing from a spring and which flowed for about a mile. Only the two hills were brown and arid. On one was the hospital, and on the other an unfinished mosque, the principal ornament of the town. Below were the *gourbis,* the tents of the natives, and still lower was the square containing the church, some French shops and the Commandant's or Governor's house. After a very difficult assault, General Pélissier had captured Laghouat in 1852. A small garrison of 1,000 men had been installed there.

49

In spite of her condition, Madame de Sonis insisted on riding beside her husband when they entered their new post. They arrived at nightfall; the African stars formed a brilliant canopy. Laghouat welcomed its new Commandant to the fire of salutes. The thunderous reception included a magnificent *fantasia*. This is an Arab dance performed on great occasions combining evolutions on horseback, gun firing and shouting—all in a rapid rhythm. The horses of the Arab chiefs bore the richest of trappings embroidered in gold. The weird chant of the women in native costume gathered on the terraces lent a fairylike atmosphere to the setting of the night, while the moon brought out the soft outlines of the white houses, the 30,000 palm trees, olive trees, the fig and many other fruit trees.

The governor's house was of sun-dried brick, with flat roof and balconies. It commanded a spacious view of the countryside and desert. To the Major's dismay, the church, which had been an old mosque, was small and poor. "I am ashamed to be better lodged than God," he wrote. The Arabs refused to set foot in their beautiful new mosque as a protestation against what they considered the profanation of the old!

Whenever Gaston entered a new post, the first visit was to his Master in the Tabernacle, the second to His minister, the pastor of the church. The third was for a community of religious, if there was one. "No one can find fault that I put God before men, and His representative before the authorities of the country."

There were happy days at Laghouat, where the family was united. If other officers merited the term of contempt, *kelb-ben-kelb,* sons of dogs, from the Moslem who were so difficult to impress, because too often they were stronger in faith, Major de Sonis soon won the title *"Moula-el-*

Dina," master in religion. This "great Marabout of the Roumis," as he was called had the courage of his convictions; he worshipped his God openly but not ostentatiously, and the Moslem, to whom religion is the whole man and who is so thoroughly imbued with his own beliefs, admired him for it. They would see him kneeling in his tent saying his rosary or the Little Office of Our Lady to fulfill his obligation as a Carmelite Tertiary. He maintained a strict fast even when on long expeditions, taking but one meal and that not until evening. "I know I had sufficient reasons for being dispensed," he answered the Vincentian missionaries at Laghouat, "but I did not want to give the Arabs occasion to think that the Moslems make a better Lent than Christians do."

Master horsemen, the Arabs were in admiration of their Commandant's superior skill, which soon became known to every one. They were amazed to see him subdue completely one of their desert steeds that no one had been able to ride before. Their enthusiasm knew no bounds while they watched him clearing every fence and obstacle, the first to pass danger spots, evidently enjoying the difficulty, and never falling from his horse.

It was not long before de Sonis was reminded that his was a post of combat. In April, 1861, several inhabitants, including an infant in the cradle, were assassinated by some Arabs at Djelfa. Notified by telegram, Gaston covered the 75 miles in the night and by dawn surprised some of the assassins before they had time to flee. He called a council of war, judged the murderers and had one shot. Galloping back to Laghouat in six hours, he sent his report to the governor at Algiers, Marshal Pélissier. A journalist, little in sympathy with the Army, still less with the religion of de Sonis, got wind of it and made a big story of the affair and agitated those who are eager to be agitated before they know the true facts about what is agitating them. The Masons were pleased. The growing fame of that monk-like officer was a thorn to them. As soldier, Pélissier approved of his Major's action—the council of war that condemned an assassin seized in the very act of the offense. His conscience reminded him of the thousand some Arabs he himself had had burned in 1845 in the grottoes in which they had taken refuge. But Pélissier was a politician. He removed Major de Sonis from the governorship of Laghouat and sent him back to his regiment at Mascara.

De Sonis had only to explain himself before Marshal Pélissier, promise more caution in future, and he would have been returned to his post of trust. But Gaston de Sonis was above disgrace. "I know the Arabs. If I do not use rigor today, they will start over again tomorrow. I consulted my conscience; my duty is to preserve the good by terrifying the evil-doers." He packed up and, without a word of complaint, returned to Mascara. "Military obedience does not argue," he said. What he felt most was the fatigue that the long and difficult journey would cause his beloved wife. Travelling was primitive in those days. His delicate attention and tenderness, above all his lofty spiritual help, strengthened her to endure the hardships until they reached Mascara. Major de Sonis proved himself as great a soldier by the silence he maintained in disgrace as by his brilliant chivalry in action. "It is hard, but I expected it. Those gentlemen at Algiers know very well, however, that I journey at my own expense!" was the only comment he allowed himself.

When they entered the post of disgrace, there was nothing to give Madame de Sonis hope that they would be leaving it soon. If Gaston was the leader, Anaïs was capable of following. Madame de Sonis fell ill, and on the 16th of July gave birth to their seventh child. It was the Feast of Our Lady of Mount Carmel and they gave the little girl the name of Marthe-Carmel. She had to pay with her life for the politicians at Algiers. Always frail, she was, nevertheless, a predestined child, and the consolation of her parents. She died when she was three years old, saying: "I want to go to Heaven!" Her death was one of the sorrows of Gaston de Sonis' life from which he never quite recovered. He seemed to hear the patter of her little feet long after she had passed away. In writing about her he feared to send "more tears than ink." Carmel de Sonis was buried in the desert where she had been born and had blossomed so briefly . . . a jewel of the flesh and bone of France's great soldier buried in the sands of the Sahara!

In the meantime, the Army had not concealed its indignation. Sonis was their pride, the exemplar of military perfection; their confidence in his loyalty could not be shaken; their admiration would not cool. Marshal Pélissier, seeing him refuse to try to get back into the good graces of the authorities, made the advance. Shaking de Sonis' hand, he said: "Come, now, Commandant, let us forget the past. You are a man of duty!" By way of reparation, he appointed him commandant of the territory of Saïda.

Saïda, to the south of Mascara, was a town founded in 1854, and belonged to the province of Oran. The commandant had to minister to 30,000 natives divided into 16 tribes and a small settlement of Europeans extending over a large territory.

"The arrival in Saïda of the Commandant and his family," related Father Lacombe, pastor of the church, "was the dawn of a religious resurrection for my parish, which needed it. Expecting to make my visit first, I found the brilliant major at my house. He said he owed the advance to the priest, the representative of God. I saw him early next morning at Mass, which he hoped to attend every day. He wanted to communicate each time, but I believed it my duty to take account of the spirit of the garrison which I had come to know by painful experience. I thought it well to restrict his Communions to two or three a week. Ever since, I have regretted having deprived that beautiful soul of the happiness of more frequent Eucharistic days—also for having deprived the Sacred Heart of Jesus of the loving adoration of a heart more completely His than any I have ever known. . . . His good example produced the effect of a mission." The church once desolate began to fill with officers and colonists. Albert de Sonis, the third son, served Mass every morning.

It was not only warlike tribes that de Sonis had to combat. He had to battle against military magistrates too loose in their laws protecting the honor of family life, and also against the libertines who set the tone by their bad example. He could expect to be removed from his post for fidelity to his duty as an honest man, as he had been removed from Laghouat for adhering to his duty as a soldier.

The reputation he had won at Laghouat as incorruptible lover of justice soon grew up around him along with a religious veneration. The Arabs called him the "great French marabout," the holy just one. The same justice was meted out to the poor Arab in his tatters as to the rich Moslem in his flowing white burnous. When they came to their governor with their complaints, they stood on equal footing.

De Sonis was not long in Saïda when a Moslem approached him to solicit the coveted post of caïd. The Commandant listened patiently until, with a sleek smile, the solicitor produced from under the folds of his burnous a bag of five-franc pieces. Major de Sonis sprang to his feet. He had the man hurled from his presence and shut up in prison, money bag and all, for two weeks for insulting his Commandant! The news of this incident soon spread among the tribes and increased everyone's admiration for his disinterestedness.

A foreign officer of high birth, who had entered the French Army, took advantage of the Commandant's absence to entertain himself and his friends by organizing an ostrich hunt. As large a number as possible of Arab horsemen was employed. A vast circle is made around the birds, narrowing by degrees. The imprisoned birds that escape being shot or knocked down fly over the circle and flee into the vastness of the desert. They are pursued by the horsemen until they or the horses drop from fatigue. An expensive game indeed!

A great number of horses died on this occasion. The officer decreed that those whose horses had survived should club together to replace those which had died. An iniquitous proposal as the value of the ostriches and their plumage sold would more than have compensated for the horses.

When Major de Sonis returned, the Arabs lost no time in lodging their complaints. After hearing the whole story, he summoned the elegant officer into his presence.

"Sir, I give you your choice of two things: either you will draw up a true and official report of your manner of acting in this matter, which I will myself forward to the General; or you will go yourself, with my Arab interpreter, who will represent me, find the horsemen whom you engaged for your ostrich hunt, and tell them that you come by my orders and in my name to repair the loss that you caused them. You will pay each Arab, on the spot, the price of the horse he has lost. Captain, which do you choose?"

The haughty officer bowed and departed. He preferred to pay with his purse rather than with his reputation . . . or something worse. When the Arabs saw him come in person to make this solemn reparation, they could not find high enough praise for their Commandant.

Gaston and Anaïs de Sonis welcomed two more children while at Saïda: Joseph in May, 1863, and Jean in December of the following year. But sorrows and joys mingled all through the life of this exemplary couple. God claimed another daughter, their little Marie-Thérèse, when she was only five years old.

Major de Sonis' letters at this time express the desire for more time to pray in solitude. He felt a need to commune with the Master Who was inundating his soul with light and grace. He trembled to think of the responsibility of corresponding to them. "God has made me see so clearly the things of the other world. He has so often enlightened me with so great a light. He has shown me the goal with such certainty, that not to follow the way is for me a great crime. . . . Pray, then, for me. . . ." "My dear Henri, nothing in this world is worth our being attached to it. God alone can fill the heart of man. To God, therefore, may we dedicate ourselves . . . and always more and more."

In April, 1863, Napoleon III declared that Algeria was not a colony but rather an Arab kingdom. "The natives, like the colonists, have an equal right to my protection. I am as much emperor of the Arabs as I am emperor of the French." For his character, qualities, and conscientiousness, Major de Sonis was designated to take part in the division and delimitation of the Arabian territory. For five months he laboured at the arduous task. "God knows better than

56

we what is good for us. I am at a good school for breaking my will and natural tastes, which so far I have not succeeded in doing."

The result of exalting the Arabs was a bloody insurrection which gained ground rapidly. The French were betrayed, assassinated along the route, and an entire company of soldiers annihilated to the last man. General Pélissier died and was succeeded by Marshal Mac-Mahon, who prepared a vigorous campaign. As Major de Sonis and his regiment were to form part of it, it was decided that Madame de Sonis should return to France with the children. The parting took place over the grave of little Marthe-Carmel, "the pearl of my family," as her father called her, "and one of the pearls in the crown that encircles the glorious head of Our Lady of Mount Carmel. . . . Our hearts were very full, but Our Lord helped us to bear the burden." He added: "The terrible massacres of our troops during this last month made me think seriously of receiving my Viaticum before starting. I have had that consolation and am ready to be buried for all eternity. I have placed myself whole-heartedly in the hands of God, Who has always been so good to me, and, borne in the arms of His Providence, I started for this desert where I am still."

A horrible spectacle met Major de Sonis and his men as they neared the site of one of the uprisings. The bodies of the French soldiers were still strewn over the sands and putrifying in the heat of the tropical sun. So violent a stench emanated from the hideous mass that even the jackals and hyenas and birds of prey no longer ventured near. De Sonis gave the order to bury the remains but the soldiers recoiled in spite of themselves. Taking up pickaxe and spade he started to dig the trench. His example was stronger than the word of command. Taking the shovel

57

from their major, the soldiers soon had buried in a common grave the horrifying remains of humanity. "I was charged to gather up what remained of the corpses of 150 of our men massacred by the Arabs," wrote de Sonis. "Among them were officers and soldiers of my regiment. I could not recognize them. However, I discovered in the middle of all those bones and scraps of flesh partly devoured by jackals what remained of a handsome young man, my comrade. That body had been the object of so much care . . . but what has become of the soul? Yes, we are souls!"

"What a man this de Sonis is, and what a Christian!" wrote his colonel, the future General Marmier. "At times we had nothing to eat but a dead horse, and yet he never broke his Friday abstinence. He is the most astounding officer of the Army!"

Major de Sonis forgot himself in his concern for others. On his part he wrote: "The Army has suffered, and still suffers much. The cold, the rain, the wind, the snow after a scorching sun, bread soon replaced by biscuits, the muddy waters of the *r'dirs*, the brackish water of desert wells, all that has passed over me without my having the least merit in withstanding it. If I need still to strengthen my faith in the supernatural, I have only to think of God's goodness towards myself." "God is always so good to me," he wrote to a Jesuit friend. "He helped me so much on this expedition. Yes, God is the good God. . . . And as I have been in the habit of meditating on death which is the friend of my profession I am often seized with a *great desire of dying for the cause of the Church.*"

Jean, his ninth child, was born at Castres while Sonis was on this expedition. He wrote to his friends at Limoges: "My wife is full of courage. She is wholly dedicated to God.

This is for me an example and a great consolation. Our union which you have known since the first days at Limoges has only increased with the years. It is founded in God." The letter quoted in the Foreword was written on this expedition. About this time his brother Théobald married an exemplary young girl.

For Major de Sonis, life in the camp was no less the life of an apostle. His letters preserve for us a beautiful example. A Jesuit friend of his at Algiers, Father de Bouchaud, had recommended to him a seventeen-year-old soldier who was making the campaign with him and whose mother back in France was anxious for news.

"I had hardly finished Father de Bouchaud's letter when I went in search of the dear child and found him squatting in his little tent. We quickly became acquainted and I brought him under my roof which is a little larger than his. There, I gave him all that was needed for writing to his mother. . . .

"Your child is so interesting, Madame, that I had no difficulty in becoming attached to him. After a few days we were like old friends, and he will tell you that I scolded him several times for not having come to me, when I would so willingly have placed myself at his disposal. Need I tell you, Madame, that I went straight to the point with him. It was all the more necessary since we are on campaign where a bullet could touch at any moment the life that is so dear to you. I was happy to find in him feelings of lively faith and it is a great consolation for me to think that God was willing to use me to revive it. We made together our examen of conscience and we arrived at Saïda with the promise of becoming better, by an altogether new way. . . . I have enrolled this dear child in the too small society of Christians that is already coming to notice in the Army.

59

In large part we are the work of the Company of Jesus, because our best recruits come from their schools."

A little later he wrote: "At the moment I am writing, Peter is here beside me, which is for me a real happiness. We attend Mass together in the morning, and he has promised not to leave Saïda before receiving Holy Communion beside his friend. I think that will be a great consolation for you and the proof that St. Joseph is a very good father and protector. He charges himself with the important thing, which is the complete conversion of our Peter. Need I tell you, Madame, that by conversion I understand a complete abandonment to God, a total gift of soul, of entire self to Jesus Christ, to His Church? This is what I want of my young friend. I thirst to see him grow and elevate himself to those spheres where the truth *is*, where the air is so pure and where it is so good to live!" Let us remind ourselves that this correspondence is not from a priestly director, but from an army officer on campaign where his military alertness was needed at every moment; it concerns a young soldier of 17, not a cloistered novice or a seminarian.

At the end of December, the campaign was over. All the tribes had submitted and the whole region of the Tell was pacified. Major de Sonis, however, was not very pleased with the results.

"It is true that the tribes have sent in their submission," he wrote, "but the repression has been so weak that I fear we shall have to begin again in the Spring. The insurrection has lasted from April to December; it greatly compromised the interests of our colonists, and changed the whole authority from civil to military hands. I think I shall be ordered to take back my command at Saïda before Christmas, but shall find myself alone there, where I was before so happy with my wife and children. . . . I hope however to keep Christmas this year as a Christian. I have fasted too long from the Eucharistic Food, and I am longing to resume my old habits, for God treats me as a spoilt child. I will be sure to remember you at the holy Table. Don't forget me."

In May, 1865, the Emperor, Napoleon III, landed at Algiers. Desiring to enter into direct relations with the Arab chiefs, he wanted an officer of distinction to accompany him, one fluent in the Arabian language and familiar with the customs of the people and one in whom they had confidence. The Emperor already had his eyes on the brilliant young cavalier who was attracting everyone's attention and he wanted to take into his military household an officer of such distinction. Marshal Mac-Mahon thought of Major de Sonis as best qualified and the most deserving of the honor. To the astonishment of everyone, Gaston declined. "You are losing your fortune. You will be general next year," objected his friends. Had he been given an order he would have obeyed, but he maintained reserve because of the Emperor's attitude towards the Papacy. "I believe I am faithful. I believe I am faithful to God, faithful to our princes, to all that merits fidelity. I believe I am faithful to my friends, who would not be mine if they were not first the friends of God. I am seized every day by a greater love for the Church, and the hatred that her cruel enemies bear her in this sad century enkindles my love more and more."

In June, 1865, Gaston de Sonis was promoted to the rank of lieutenant-colonel to the 1st Spahis. He was preparing to spend his vacation with his wife and children at Castres and had gone as far as Oran when he received the order to go to Laghouat as commandant. Bitter experience had constrained the authorities to give him back, with a higher grade, the post they took from him four years before. Gaston de Sonis had been disgraced for the execution of one bandit; now there were hundreds of them. The massacre of settlers and travellers multiplied. The authorities counted on de Sonis to re-establish peace and order. Full reparation was made to him at last, to the great satisfaction of the Army.

The Ouled-Sidi-Cheikh was the most formidable of the tribes that had refused submission. They grouped around them less powerful tribes that Islamism bound to them as allies in a common and fanatical hatred of the Christian. Preferring their nomadic, impoverished life to the civilization offered them by the French, these tribes wandered about with their lean flocks in search of pasturage and water, with no shelter but their poor tents and no home but the vastness of the desert. They had at their head a chief of renown, Si-Lalla, a real warrior, and his 20-year-old nephew, Si-Hamed. When a marabout in the name of Allah preached a "holy war" the effect on the surrounding tribes was like a spark igniting a barrel of gunpowder. They would run to arms, pillage, ravage, and massacre the French settlers and soldiers. Just as suddenly, they would disappear into their unknown and inaccessible solitudes.

In October, 1865, de Sonis' forebodings were justified: an insurrection broke out in every direction. He studied the nature of war in that desert country and prepared his offensive. His use of the camel for transportation of baggage, provisions, and water supply was one of the most useful organizations of his administration in Africa.

From October to December the column was employed in various small expeditions against hostile tribes. In December it was reported that Si-Lalla had made a raid on a tribe friendly to the French at Metlili, which was about 125 miles south of Laghouat at the extreme frontier of the French colony. It was a wretched little place, built in a sandy ravine. The rugged cliffs surrounding it served as ramparts. When the French arrived, peace was offered on condition that the immense spoils of camels and flocks that had been carried off be returned. The answer was a sharp fire.

De Sonis started at once with his cavalry, two companies of Infantry and of Zouaves, and after a quarter of an hour's march discovered, on his left, insurgents on the heights above the valley. The Infantry instantly began to scale the rocks on hands and feet and fell on the enemy, dislodging them before they had time to prepare for this attack, while the Cavalry made a charge on their right. Then began a pursuit from rock to rock. The enemy fled in all directions leaving their dead on the route. Colonel de Sonis noticed at his left a troop of insurgents fleeing rapidly, driving the stolen flocks before them. Leaving his Infantry with the order to join him as soon as possible, he went in their pursuit. The insurgents, believing themselves safe amidst the rocks as inaccessible to horses, mocked and insulted him. De Sonis had his men dismount, and leaving only a few to guard the horses, gave the order to open fire. The enemy scattered, abandoning the flocks and herds. Very soon the whole of the French troops reassembled and they returned victoriously to Metlili at half past seven in the evening. They brought back thousands of sheep and several hundred camels. It was due to the strategem and prudence of their Commander that the French won the day and did not lose a single man or suffer even one seriously injured soldier. To teach the people a lesson, de Sonis assembled them in the mosque, laid on them a fine of 100,000 francs, and replaced their Caïds who had gone over to the enemy. He liberated the Negro slaves and took some of them back with him to Laghouat. He had them placed with good families where they would be instructed in the Catholic religion.

Learning that a great Arab chief was at a distance of only four days' march, de Sonis was tempted to go there, but the instructions he had received did not permit him to go that far from Metlili. He knew that not to crush the insurgents now would mean trouble later on. Another victory would bring glory to his name, and his family would benefit. But de Sonis was above every consideration except duty. His duty was to obey: so with his entire regiment he returned to Laghouat on January 28, 1866, where his wife and children soon joined him. He was not to taste for long the joys of family life that were so sweet to him.

CHAPTER VI

An Expedition into the Desert

On March 16th, Si-Hamed, the fanatic nephew of Si-Lalla, marched on Géryville and killed or wounded some 60 soldiers of a detachment of the French garrison. De Sonis organized an expedition and departed on March 25, 1866. As was his custom before leaving on campaign, he first received his Eucharistic Master, surrounded by his men. The account of this expedition which comprised 3,000 men and nearly 2,000 camels, was recorded by an eye-witness, a lieutenant of de Sonis. The objective was to intercept Si-Lalla before he could join forces with another rebel chief, Ben-Naceur, who held that part of the country to the south called Mzab.

For days, under broiling sun, the column pushed its way forward, cantoning at night by a *r'dir*, a desert pool of yellow, briny, sun-heated water. The greatest enemy of the Sahara was not the Arab but thirst. The rivers indicated on the maps could not be depended on as the sun would leave them beds of dried-up mud. The *r'dirs* could be exhausted at one draught by a caravansary. The only dependable source was the wells existing from antiquity, but these were at several days' march from one another. The supply of water carried on an expedition was of primary importance, and the water skins were filled at these ancient wells.

A whirlwind stirred up the sand, clouding the sky and enveloping the column so thoroughly that one's nearest neighbor could not be seen. The scorching sand blinded the eyes and parched the throat. The hurricane lasted two hours, then diminished in violence, leaving delicate arabesques formed by the sand on the soil. As soon as the storm subsided, the colonel made a hasty roll call. One soldier did not answer. De Sonis had the plain searched as far as the horizon, and sent out a party of horsemen who were not more successful. He ordered fires of brushwood to burn through the entire night, but the unfortunate man never returned nor was any trace of his body ever found.

At cantonment, the colonel saw to everyone's installation and was activity itself in supervising every detail down to the distribution of the meagre rations. Before taking a few hours of sleep wrapped in his sheepskin, he consecrated a large part of the time to communing with his Master, Who also had known prayer-filled nights in a desert. It was during this time, taken from sleep, that he would converse with a young officer commended to his apostolate by the Vincentian Fathers. By the end of the expedition, one more soul was the conquest of Miles Christi's zeal. The first to rise, de Sonis made his meditation and prayer again a long time in the profound silence of the desert under the canopy of the brilliant firmament.

The heat increased until it became infernal, drying up in a few hours the springs that had contained some water the day previous. The terrible enemy of the desert—thirst—was tracking down the men. On they marched in the silence of death, without so much as a tree, a tuft of grass or a tiny stream to revive life or change the monotony of the landscape. Now and again a little row of hills appeared in the distance, giving them hope of finding a rock or a ravine; but, deception. The nearer they came, the quicker the mirage disappeared. Man and beast began to fall. Not to discourage the Infantry, de Sonis and the other officers dismounted and walked on foot over the burning sands.

The largest share of the sufferings fell on de Sonis who bore everything his troops had to endure with the greatest cheerfulness. He would take no complaints such as the length of the day's march. A soldier in a bad humor grumbled that it was all very well for the colonel to let his men die of hunger, while he himself enjoyed a capital meal. The complaint reached de Sonis who invited the man to dine with him the next day. Rather confused at the honor conferred upon him, the soldier consoled himself by the thought of soon having a good dinner. Evening came. He went into his chief's tent; both of them squatted on a mat. The dinner was served: 2 biscuits, 2 portions of watery rice (what soldiers call rice cooked in its juice), and a ration of lukewarm water in a goatskin. It was the daily "menu" of the chief and his guest received the same. This incident soon made the rounds. Everyone laughed but no more complaints were made.

Whenever the expeditionary force seemed to be over-taking the enemy, they would find the encampment deserted. That warrior of the desert—Si-Lalla—had evaded them once more, having penetrated deeper into the trackless sand wastes. The men and horses were falling more from thirst than from fatigue; they could go no farther. No one could have foreseen such infernal heat, and the officers had only praise for the wisdom, courage, and prudence with which their colonel had organized the expedition. But de Sonis felt the full weight of the responsibility of those several thousand lives, and he prayed for a miracle.

He sent some dependable Arab scouts of a tribe loyal to the French in search of the enemy. The soldiers considered it a miracle when they returned with an immense booty taken from Si-Lalla.

There was still the need of water. The soldiers were disputing over the drops squeezed from the mud wrung in their handkerchiefs. De Sonis never felt anguish more cruel, but he never lost his calm nor his confidence in God. He committed himself to his protector, St. Joseph, and prayed with agony in his heart. The Arabs sent to search for the springs returned at the same moment to report there was water in wells only six miles distant. It was the salvation of the men. They believed they owed it to the prayer of their colonel. A soldier expressed the sentiment of that column of Frenchmen when he said: "Never did I believe a day would come when a cup of water would mean more to me than a cup of wine!"

Refreshed with new life, the horses trotted without urging and the hearts of all were light in the anticipation of overtaking Si-Lalla who, according to the scouts, was encamped not far away. When the cavalry reached the spot, there was no trace of his tents. The colonel was faced with the grave menace of discouragement. A thousand thoughts were turning themselves over in his mind: should they press forward, not knowing where they were going? Would they reach the next well before complete exhaustion? The horses were already falling; the heat was increasing; the supply of water was giving out. None of this mental torture showed exteriorly. De Sonis prayed for light to know his duty to God, to France, to his men; and God made him understand that his duty was to stop. Risking the possibility of being considered for the first time wanting in courage, with death in his heart, he gave the command to stop the march. Sonis had already proved and was again and again to prove his daring and courage, but he was never foolhardy nor imprudent about the lives of those for whom he was responsible. The column had endured so much to come this near to success, but the exhausted condition of the men spelt death, and Sonis was, above all, a man of duty. A less conscientious leader would have risked sacrificing his men to glorify his own name.

While the column started on the return march, de Sonis sent a party of Arab guides with two companies of soldiers on camels to pursue the enemy. This time Si-Lalla had difficulty escaping with his life. He had to leave behind so many of his possessions that southern Algeria could expect several years of tranquility and peace.

On May 2, 1866, the expeditionary force returned to Laghouat. The final success of the campaign that lasted six weeks was justly attributed to the wisdom and unconquerable energy of Gaston de Sonis. There is food for thought in these lines penned to a friend:

"We suffered much in the Sahara; but such hardships are singularly profitable to the soul, as well as to the body, and the former *has more to gain from bad fortune than from good*. The human result of it to me is the Cross of Officer of the Legion of Honor, which I shall place at the feet of Our Lady of Africa at Algiers." The reward received after the Italian Campaign he gave to Our Lady of Victories in Paris.

CHAPTER VII

Hero of the Home

∿∿∿∿∿∿∿∿∿∿∿∿∿∿∿∿∿∿∿∿∿∿∿∿∿∿∿∿∿∿∿∿∿∿∿∿∿

Four and a half years more of our hero's life were to be spent in Africa. For a while he would know comparative peace and the consolations of home life. Every spring he made an excursion into the South for a twofold reason: to keep the soldiers in shape, and to remind the Arabs that the French were not sleeping at their post—an important matter. Apart from this, it is easy to follow the order of his day which was recorded by an aide-de-camp.

"I was struck by the activity of his life, the order and decorum that reigned in it. Everything was regulated as in the life, I will not say of a soldier, but of a monk." He rose early, made his prayer in a room apart, meditating on a chapter of the Gospels or of *The Imitation*. "At halfpast six, he went to Mass in silence. I accompanied him. Sometimes while crossing the square, I would make some joke, which made him smile; but he used to reprove me afterwards, saying that the Mohametans were always serious, when they went to their prayers and that my childish gaiety would seem irreverent to them." After a quick breakfast, there was the reception of French officers or Arab chiefs. At 9 o'clock he drew up his report. After lunch, at 11 a.m., he would recreate in the garden with his wife and children, then go horseback riding into the limitless desert that held a fascination for his contemplative spirit. Around 2:30, he would study in his office some military work on the development of mechanized warfare and the effect of its progress on the branch of the army that held his greatest interest—the cavalry. Or again, he would refresh himself with some spiritual book. This would take till supper. He spent little time at his meals and ate frugally, making the excuse that his was "the stomach of an ostrich." The evening was given to his family: conversation, the Little Office of Our Lady which he said to fulfill his obligation as a tertiary of Carmel, rosary in common, and family night prayers. When someone expressed surprise how he managed to give such a good part of his time to God when his activity was well known, he explained simply: "God multiplies time for those who serve Him and an early rising advances many things."

Let us pause a minute and *think*.

We must streamline our devotions in order to keep pace with the rush that *must* be cramped into our day. Consequently, our activity lacks foundation and is little more than "beating the air." The poor human heart, starved for the food for which it was made, stops dead in protest of this abuse—or misuse. Doctors call it heart attack or heart failure. "Thou has made us for Thyself, O Lord, and our heart is restless until it rests in Thee," diagnoses Saint Augustine, the great Doctor of Africa.

Those who accomplish the most in the world are the contemplatives, because they seek first the Kingdom of God and His justice. A contemplative who does not work is not contemplating but is stagnating in a torpor of self-absorption. Do we realize the import of the new Feast of Saint Joseph the Worker? Saint Teresa of Avila, the great mystic and contemplative, tells her daughters of Carmel that works, good works alone, are the children of the Spiritual Marriage. Human activity is worth nothing for Heaven. It is worse than nothing when inspired by the devil. Of this, we have much proof before our eyes in the ravages made by Communism. When a human being concentrates his activity on mastering himself and being an instrument of God, no one can measure the stature he attains nor the horizon of his influence for good. It is in prayer, in communing with the Guest of the soul in grace, that light comes to the mind to direct activity, and love to the heart to give it life. There are graces which come only through prayer. How often our Holy Father, Pope Pius XII, has stressed the necessity of prayer! Houses of prayer are keeping the world from destruction today, but every Catholic in the world should remember that he is "the temple of God" and that His house must be a house of prayer. Saint Teresa of Avila said if anyone has no one to teach him to pray, let him go to the glorious Saint Joseph. Saint Joseph the Worker, teach us to pray! And anyone who wants to order his day better, to know how to put prayer, or more of it, into his life, has only to study the life of Miles Christi.

Gaston de Sonis' religion was above all practical. He knew that before he could do good to others he had to work at his own sanctification, and he knew that it is not what one does but what one is that is the important thing. His guide, his model, was the Heart of his Master. His ardent devotion consisted not in pictures and badges but in returning love for love. Every day he renewed his Consecration to the Sacred Heart. It was to imitate the Master that he wanted to be and to remain poor, that he accepted with calm and resignation the continual sacrifices, crosses and humiliations that fidelity to his profession offered him or that came directly from the hand of God. His was an ardent and impetuous nature, and he had a quick, hot temper—a French temper, if you like. It gave him many a struggle but he mastered both his nature and his temper by learning of *his Master,* meek and humble of heart, and by using the means that Mother Church puts into the hands of all her children.

He was always trying to learn greater calmness in his ways and actions, and to acquire the virtues in which he thought himself deficient. His chief of staff at one time records that Colonel de Sonis made on him the impression of being the most well-bred gentleman he had ever known. He had to go to his colonel every morning to receive his orders, transmit them to the camp, and then see to their execution. He was always received kindly and with a charming graciousness, "When things went wrong, he was very much annoyed and his first words showed it, although they were always perfectly courteous," relates this officer. "But then, overcoming this first impulse of vexation or anxiety, he always fixed his eyes on something behind his table, where he was sitting. One day I had to go around this writing-table and there I discovered the object that brought back his sweetness and calm—a Crucifix!"

It was Gaston's custom to kneel whenever the Blessed Sacrament was carried ostensibly to the sick. One day on such an occasion, a young girl passing in an open carriage laughed at the officer kneeling in the street. "So that makes you laugh, does it!" he flung at her, indignant of the disrespect shown his Eucharistic Master. The girl turned pale and passed on, while Gaston sought a priest to cool off, and regained his peace of soul in confession.

Another time he was at the officers' club, where he would

spend an hour from time to time through a sense of duty. He was sitting apart near the window, reading the paper, when the tinkling of a bell seemed to announce the approach of the Blessed Sacrament. There was a momentary struggle: should he kneel before all those officers? Then the thought flashed through his mind: if the emperor or the flag passed by, all these officers would stand and give their salute. The next instant he was on both knees. He glanced down to see the dilapadated wagon of a peddler pass under the window. How gaily Sonis would relate this incident!

A keen observer of discipline, he always admired those who practised it with the greatest exactness. His spirit of equity was proverbial; and seeing how highly he esteemed the profession of a soldier, the men were still more disposed to honor or at least to respect his profession of a Christian. His orders were given in a firm, precise but always very courteous manner. He rarely judged his neighbor, but if he had to, he always distinguished between character and talent. No matter how remarkable the latter might be in a man, he never could be brought to admire him if he were mean or unjust. Injustice of any sort was odious to him. He appreciated above all kindness, indulgence, the pardon of injuries.

"He was very young in character," wrote an aide-de-camp, "loving the young officers and taking great interest in us and encouraging us in every way. He liked us to be well-dressed and smart and particular about our uniforms. He loved good horses, too, and was an excellent judge of them. He invested all things connected with his profession with a charm peculiar to himself."

His trips from Laghouat to Algiers in 2 or 3 days were the amazement of everyone. He had relays of horses on the road, and would gallop the whole way, day and night, taking only a little coffee and bread on the way. One of these flying trips was made to save the Sons and Daughters of St. Vincent de Paul. Besides the two Fathers who served the church, there were four Sisters of Charity who had a little school in Laghouat, to which the Arabs were sending their children, much to de Sonis' delight. Because of difficulties between the government and the Papacy at that time, the Superior General of the Vincentians was going to recall his Religious. Colonel de Sonis flew to Algiers, where he pleaded before the civil, military and ecclesiastical authorities with success. To the Vincentian Fathers who had begged him not to compromise his official position, he replied: "I always set the bow of my ship towards the good God; whatever the winds, I keep to my course, for, after all, it is only at that port that I wish to land."

Sonis would not tolerate girls loitering near the precincts of the camp. He had the police intercept convoys coming from Algiers with girls of ill fame. He was hated for this intolerance . . . but by whom? So great was the secret veneration for his uprightness, however, that even those who detested him, expected miracles from his holiness. To give one example: the troops were returning from the annual expedition into the South. The detachment spread out over the dried bed of a torrent for several kilometres. The bed was over half a mile wide. The sky clouded over the mountains, announcing the sudden approach of a storm. In that country it would be but a matter of a moment for the dried bed to be transformed into an overflowing torrent. The provisions and supplies were on the opposite bank. There was only the one way to reach them. Could they make it? In this crisis of cruel anguish, de Sonis jumped from his horse and knelt on the bank to pray with his whole heart to St. Joseph, protector of the Holy Family. The last man and last camel had scarcely reached the bank when the torrent roared down from the mountain, sweeping everything in its course as so much chaff. Little wonder that the soldiers whispered "a miracle."

Laghouat appealed to Gaston so much that he would willingly have remained there the rest of his life, if his family could be with him. His sensitive nature suffered less from the conflict of opinions and political disturbances in that remote and picturesque retreat. Laghouat was the birthplace of three more children. Germaine, the tenth, arrived on June 1, 1866, just one month after de Sonis returned from the expedition into the Sahara recorded in the previous chapter. This child was going to be a June rose for the Heart of the Master and a consolation for her father.

François, the sixth son, arrived the following year and for months was at the point of death. Three times he was thought dead. "I gave him all my tears," wrote the poor father. The parents shared the night watching over the child. Neither fatigue nor anxiety dispensed Sonis from any of his military duties. The baby was cured after he had put on it a relic of Saint Philomena, a cure the doctor declared "extraordinary." In gratitude, the twelfth and last child, born February 16, 1869, was given the name Philomène.

Sonis was not less vigilant as a father than he was alert as a soldier. He taught his children to use all the beauties of nature to lift their minds to the Creator. He showed them the brilliant African stars and taught them their names and the constellations. He supervised their studies, and when the boarders were home for the summer vacations, he tutored them in their Latin, mathematics and

GASTON DE SONIS, AT 57, TAKEN AT LIMOGES

AERIAL VIEW OF THE VILLAGE OF LOIGNY-LA-BATAILLE

SOUVENIRS OF THE BAT-
TLE OF LOIGNY IN THE
MUSEUM ADJOINING THE
CHURCH

CROSS MARKING THE SPOT WHERE GENERAL DE SONIS LAY ALL NIGHT (DECEMBER 2-3, 1870) ON THE BATTLEFIELD OF LOIGNY

STATUE OF THE SACRED HEART ERECTED ON THE BATTLEFIELD OF LOIGNY

MEMORIAL CHAPEL DEDICATED TO THE SACRED HEART
LOIGNY-LA-BATAILLE

IN THE CRYPT OF THE
CHURCH OF LOIGNY. THE
TOMB OF GENERAL GAS-
TON DE SONIS. THE TOMB
OF GENERAL DE CHA-
RETTE (LEFT)

ENTRANCE TO THE CAR-
MEL FOUNDED BY MOTH-
ER GERMAINE OF JESUS,
DAUGHTER OF GENERAL
DE SONIS, AT VERDUN,
FRANCE

CLOISTER OF THE CARMEL
OF VERDUN

history. It was a moving scene to see all the children line up at night before their father to receive his blessing on their forehead before going to bed.

Marie finished her studies at the Academy of the Sacred Heart in Poitiers in 1868 and became the little mistress of the younger children. She confided to her parents her desire to be a Carmelite, but it was on another altar that she consecrated herself to God a few years later.

De Sonis would have been happy had God chosen all his children for His service, leaving no trace of his name on earth. It would have been his privilege, his honor. He wanted his sons to be priests or soldiers, but he left them full liberty to choose. None of them became priests, but all six sons entered the military academy.

"All my thoughts are concentrated on the future of my children," he wrote to Louis de Sèze. "I do not know what they will become. I firmly believe that God will give them bread, because I do not have it to give them. But I am concerned only with seeing them faithful to God, to the traditions I shall leave them." Then this sentence worthy of a saint:

"I would rather know them to be reduced to poverty and see them die of privation than know them to be not even irreligious, but just indifferent. And still, God knows how I love them! What is life compared to eternity?" If all fathers could endorse this sentence, how different would be our juvenile problems! "I endeavor to inspire my children with my sentiments, and I hope they will be faithful to all I have loved and served."

One of the greatest joys the heart of this father experienced at this time was a letter from his second son, Henri, boarder at the Jesuit school at Poitiers, asking his permission to join the Pontifical Zouaves.

"My beloved child, you have sent me as a New Year's gift (1867) all that I could desire: a letter that made sweet tears flow, and bears witness that your heart beats in unison with your father's. . . . You had not told me that you loved God passionately, that all that is noble, beautiful, could make your young soul thrill. . . . Your dear letter which I have so often reread tells me, my Henri, that you have heard God's voice. Oh! may He be blessed a thousand times, this God so good!"

Then the great word of consent:

"Yes, I give you my permission to depart for Rome, to increase that sacred battalion, where the ancient French honor is today reborn in her youth.

"You are not yet 15. . . . My father went to war at 14 and I believe you worthy of him.

"While awaiting your departure, do what your ancestors did. In olden times, when a gentleman was to become a knight, he prepared by fast and prayer to receive the arms that he was to bear for the defense of religion, of the widow, the orphan, of right and of all that is just and sacred in this world. . . . My child, you are going to serve the greatest cause here below, because it is the cause of the Vicar of Jesus Christ. Prepare yourself for such an honor. . . ."

Henri was refused because of his age, but we shall meet him again, stamped with the likeness of his incomparable father.

The name of Gaston de Sonis was attracting more and more notice in France where his military genius was the topic of the papers. He was quoted in the seminaries and given to the aspirants to the priesthood as a model. It was natural that his sons at the boarding school in Poitiers should feel proud of their father. Sonis wrote to the Jesuit in charge: "Truly, I do not understand this pride. I possess no fortune. If I die, my children will have to gain their bread by the sweat of their brow. My forefathers may have been something in times gone by, but that was a long time ago. . . . Besides being always a detestable thing, pride must rest on something, or else ridicule is added to ugliness.

"Tell that dear child that the smaller he makes himself the more I will love him. May my son be thoroughly persuaded that there is only one thing truly important: to love God!

"I want my sons to have the benefit of good religious teaching. The general ignorance of religion at the present day is shameful and many men fall by the wayside because they do not know enough about their religion. Looking upon it simply from the human point of view, our religion is the finest philosophical doctrine there is. Should any less time be spent studying the Holy Scriptures than Plato or Aristotle?"

"I hold to it very much that my sons be distinguished. I want them to give a good impression of their education by their language, their behaviour, so that they will in this way make attractive their religion, their teachers, and the name they have received from their fathers."

An epidemic of cholera passed over the little colony in the summer of 1867 claiming many victims. The crops failed before harvest, due to an implacable drought, and the flocks perished. To add to the general misery, a plague of grasshoppers swept the country in droves so thick that they were crushed underfoot in numbers too great to be disposed of before they infected the atmosphere with disease. As many as 63 coffins were seen being taken to a cemetery at one time. The natives went so far as to eat human flesh in their hunger. "We are assisting at a frightful spectacle," wrote the Commandant of Laghouat, "famine in all its horrible details, appalling conditions such as I never knew except in books and which I took for exaggeration. Our poor Arabs die everywhere of misery and famine; we find their bodies on the roads, under tents, really everywhere! Charity multiplies under every form, without its efforts being more than a drop in the ocean. As for me, after doing all I can, I suffer cruelly from my impotence." The poor natives were to Gaston de Sonis like a family of children. How one man with restricted means could perform so much charity is one of the secrets of Heaven.

He had a friend of his own stature in the Archbishop, Charles Lavigerie, later to become Cardinal Archbishop of Carthage. This prelate opened an orphanage which soon mothered a thousand native children. Sonis stood in admiration of this charity and took great interest in the orphans. He wrote to Madame de Sèze: "We do not know the sufferings of hunger. . . . Things came to such a state here that a woman ate her child. How frightful to think of! I believe we shall be judged very severely, we who are so disposed to complain of our small trials and who always have our bread to eat. This thought should help us to support with joy the little mortifications which the Church imposes on us during this holy time of Lent. They are light compared to those endured with so much courage by these unfortunate Moslems. Pray, Madame, that Our Lord will enlighten their darkness, for there is no doubt that once Christian, this people would serve God very differently from those bastard nations of Europe who have no more faith than courage."

On his part, Cardinal Lavigerie wrote of de Sonis: "I knew, loved and admired him. . . . He shared my faith in

France's mission to the native Moslems and the pagans of the interior. He encouraged my hopes. One day I saw him in a flood of tears listening to our orphans of the famine singing the '*Ave Maris Stella*'." As member of the Congregation of Rites, Cardinal Lavigerie, on learning of de Sonis' death, was to express his desire to see the Cause for the Beatification of the saintly commandant of Laghouat introduced at Rome.

When Archbishop Lavigerie sent a nucleus of Jesuit missionaries to Laghouat for the purpose of converting the Moslems, they were welcomed with open arms by the Commandant. "With true joy I saw these good Fathers arrive," he wrote. "I have a very particular affection and veneration for them. It seems to me the spirit of God is with this Company, always attacked, always calumniated and persecuted. . . . God be blessed for sending us these holy sons of Saint Ignatius!"

Since de Sonis departed her shores, the soil of Africa has drunk the blood of the sons and daughters of France. The lives of missionaries, men and women, have been consumed in heroic sacrifices in numbers sufficient to make "waters break out in the desert and streams in the wilderness." Thirsty lands have budded forth blossoms that will bloom on the altars of the Church, and others that will keep their fragrance for the Eternal Unfolding. Perhaps the sufferings and prayers of Miles Christi, the humble servant and soldier of France, have been the seeds of many of these blossoms sown in a "land that was desolate and impassable," but which shall bud forth and "flourish like the lily."

We have already seen how faithful and pure was de Sonis' friendship. It seemed to grow deeper and purer with the years. While at Limoges, he made a pact with the family of Henri Lamy de la Chapelle that the de Sonis family would say the rosary for them on the 27th of every month, and Henri's family would do the same for the de Sonises. Ten years later he wrote from Laghouat: "My dear Henri, you know that on that day (July 27) I will be particularly united with you through the recitation of the rosary."

In his prayers he united the children of Louis de Sèze with his own to make one spiritual family. "Let us agree to make our Communion of the first Friday of each month for the intention of all these dear children and for this *intention alone* that they become fervent Christians."

The union between Gaston and Anaïs de Sonis can be given to the world as a model for those united in wedlock. The want of stability in the marriage state and the want of fidelity to the marriage promises so frequent today can find a remedy in these words written eighteen years after receiving the holy Sacrament of Matrimony. "In His goodness, God does not cease to bless our union. Our bonds which daily grow closer are in God and for God. . . . Every day is one more link in the chain that unites us. Our mutual love is more and more solid, because it reposes in love for God. So few understand and love each other as we do. . . . Pray for my beloved wife and dear children. They all love the Church and that is for me a great consolation. I have never asked of God either honors or fortune. All I desire is that my children be fervent Christians." "God alone is worthy of our end. We must raise ourselves, lift ourselves to those happy regions to love there in all liberty and purity these dear ones of our home, so worthy of holding the largest place in our heart, after God." What a great thing is the heart of a saint!

De Sonis could support with patience and resignation all the trials God sent him except one. His brother's attitude toward religion was intolerable to him. Théobald was not hostile, but indifferent. Gaston prayed for years and had others pray. One morning the brothers met accidentally outside the Church of Our Lady of Victories. Gaston had just received Holy Communion for Théobald's conversion. The brothers parted. Urged by an interior impulse, Théobald entered the church and made his peace with God. The brothers met again later that morning and Théobald, throwing himself into Gaston's arms, told him the great news. The latter wrote of it to his friends: "You know that my brother for a long time remained away from the Sacraments. Today he belongs completely to God. It is a grace that I attribute to the prayers of my Carmelite sisters."

His correspondence with a near relative, a companion of his childhood who became a religious, is remarkable, considering that it comes from a military man on constant duty, often writing from some bivouac. "I have never ceased to watch over you in heart and in prayer, because you are very dear to me. Every day belong more completely to Him Who wants to be loved without division. . . . We are the only ones who really know what true happiness is. The world does not know it." "Do not stop! Walk always in the royal way of the Cross, following that Bridegroom Who has done so much for you." "Let us seek our good God in the depth of our heart, you in your retreat and I in mine, for all agitated as it is, my life resembles yours, which would have been my choice, had God judged me worthy."

In January, 1869, the call of the bugle again broke in on this happy family life. Si-Lalla and a nephew, Si-Kaddour, "preached a holy war". Massacres multiplied all along the French frontiers. Laghouat was menaced. The

Commandant armed the loyal tribes and organized an expedition. He could take only a light detachment of 1,000 soldiers, as the Infantry had to remain to protect Laghouat. Sonis marched against three dissident marabouts—one Frenchman to four Arabs! Moreover, he had to leave Madame de Sonis in a critical condition. "Our separation was particularly bitter," wrote de Sonis, "because I left my wife very ill. She was persuaded that she was bidding me good-bye for the last time. The human heart has depths of suffering that are unfathomable."

Si-Lalla pompously announced that after he destroyed the French column he would march on Laghouat, Djelfa, and Bou Saïda—in other words, he would conquer the whole of the south of Algeria. Victory was in his train. Even the friends of France believed defeat was certain for de Sonis' little army. The *goums* were Arab horsemen that every subjugated tribe was obliged to furnish the French Army. They were drawn to the French colors by the love of warfare and the hope of booty. Mounted on their swift steeds and armed by the French, they rendered invaluable services by their extraordinary sagacity and their knowledge of the country and people. Preceding the column by 15 or more miles, they acted as guides and spies, pointing out the *r'dirs*, furnishing information and lending their support. By his kindness, justice and piety, de Sonis, their superior in horsemanship, had won their esteem and confidence, and what is more rare, their fidelity. He could always count on them. The *goums* he sent on reconnaissance returned to report on Si-Lalla's strength and position. Pressing de Sonis' hand, they exclaimed: "Tomorrow, Commander, we will die by your side!"

On February 1st, the French troops marched to the attack. They were formed in a square. All were to fight on foot, but in case the enemy broke the square the cavalry was to charge. "We were to march closely and slowly like a fortress," wrote de Sonis, "and not to stop till we reached the enemy's bivouac. The lack of numbers was to be supplied by our tactics and solidity. . . . Organized and armed as we were, defending the soil of our new country, we might say we represented civilization against barbarians."

After about an hour's march, they heard the tread of the enemy's infantry advancing towards them. Just then they found themselves in a deep valley, surrounded by rocky hills. It had but one passage, which was only about 60 yards wide. They found the enemy already in possession of it and waiting there for them, while the enemy's cavalry crowned the heights on either side. To his right, de Sonis saw another valley but it was separated from him by a line of rocky hills. It was their only chance of safety, but how to arrive there without being intercepted? Calling together the chiefs of the detachments, he ordered that at his signal, when the drums and clarions would sound the charge, every man was to scale the hill and there establish himself promptly and definitely. He continued the march towards the pass to within 60 yards of the enemy, who shouted their triumphant hurrahs at seeing the troops fall into their trap. De Sonis gave the signal; there was a sudden turn to the right. The movement was executed with such rapidity and in such perfect unison that in a few moments the square crowned the heights and had reformed themselves in a very strong position on the slopes of the hills commanding both valleys. At the summit there was a plateau about 10 feet wide, where Lieutenant-Colonel de Sonis took up his position to direct his troops. Alone mounted, he made a fine target for the Arabs, but the very sight of their leader had a magnetic influence on his men. The enemy's first impulse at this sudden move was to draw back. They then formed themselves again, and surrounded the French army, attacking on four sides at once. The Arab cavalry charged furiously; their action was really splendid. They sprang forward sometimes alone, sometimes in groups. There was a critical moment when victory seemed inevitably theirs, when a space was made in the square. The French cavalry charged the vulnerable point and the Arab infantry fled under the heavy fire. Si-Lalla tried to harangue them but his voice was unheard. The last to yield sprang to their horses and disappeared into the desert, a cloud of dust marking their flight. The Arabs lost several hundred dead or wounded, which they left behind; the French had 10 wounded and no dead. This was known as the battle of Ain Madhi. A colonel wrote:

"Thanks to Colonel de Sonis' perfect understanding of war in the Sahara, thanks to his brilliant and audacious energy, to his chivalrous bravery, to the rapidity of his thought and decisions, to his happy choice of defensive position, to his sure-sightedness, thanks also to his remarkable composure in difficult moments, to the prestige he exercises over the natives as well as the troops . . . the victory was complete." On his side, de Sonis wrote in praise of his men: "Each one did his duty. These are the only words fitting for the French troops. Everyone believed we were lost, and that multitude hailed us with frantic hurrah, the cry of cannibals. God fought for us; it was wonderful to see silence in the midst of deafening cries, order in the midst of disorder, with the cannon for our only music. It was one of the most stirring moments of my life."

For her part, Madame de Sonis, although so near death, was bearing like a soldier the part that falls to women and those behind the lines in time of war. "Although the distance was great," she recorded, "we heard the cannon. The day passed in mortal anguish; prayer was my only consolation. God must also have given my dear husband the calm so necessary in these moments, because, better than anyone, he saw the danger that threatened his family. He knew that once victors, the enemy would attack Laghouat, deprived of troops, and would have killed us all. The following night, towards dawn, a cavalier brought me a letter from my husband announcing the victory, but at the same time saying that he was leaving in pursuit of Si-Lalla."

The exhausted troops returned to Laghouat on February 12, where their colonel was received as a saviour. Marshal Mac-Mahon highly praised de Sonis in his report. The Secretary of War glorified "the brave Colonel de Sonis, one of the most exemplary men of the Army, for his bravery as well as for his qualities as father of the family." A military triumph was organized and the victor was covered with glory. Napoleon III sent him as homage his *Life of Caesar* (Life of Napoleon I) and promoted him to the rank of colonel to the 6th Regiment of Chasseurs.

Four days later, Madame de Sonis gave birth to their twelfth and last child: Philomène. The proud father wrote: "We gave her in baptism the name of this dear Saint to whom we have very special devotion, owing to all the graces obtained through her intercession." Anaïs was 38, Gaston 43.

Sonis himself fell sick after this campaign. During his enforced retreat of silence, his spiritual life deepened still more. "I belong to God more and more, not only 'up to the neck,' as Father de Ravignan used to say, but over head and ears. When one sets out to love God, one cannot love Him enough. In spite of that, I am always the useless servant you know so well."

In April, Sonis was sent to Aumale, a strategic position of the first order, demanding of the governor the talents of a soldier as well as of an administrator. Aumale is southeast of Algiers and in 1869 counted 6,000 inhabitants.

Laghouat paid their Commandant a moving farewell. Sonis was loved and revered not only by the French population, but by the Moslems and natives as well.

The move to Aumale was the last one de Sonis was to make in Africa. He had a little tribe now all his own to lead, which he did with the abandonment of a Moses leading the Israelites in the desert, as Jean des Marets picturesquely puts it. Madame de Sonis was on the way to recovery. Political events menacing Europe clouded the stay at the new post. The storm would surely break at any time. In spite of it, the Vatican Council was preparing the definition of the Infallibility of the Pope. Sonis was too humble to pretend to be a theologian, but his love for the Church and right sense of orthodoxy set him on the side of his friend, Cardinal Pie of Poitiers, a valiant champion of Infallibility. His letters felicitate the Cardinal for being "associated with the greatest work of this century." "How happy would I be if one day I could kneel at the feet of Pius IX and beg the blessing of this holy Pontiff for my whole family! It seems to me I would then be assured that my children would never betray the great cause of the Church, for which I would die." Sonis was anticipating with joy the definition of the dogma when Marshal Mac-Mahon visited him in Aumale and announced as good news the probability of war with Prussia. Sonis astonished everyone by stating that France was not ready "either morally or materially."

Events grew rapidly worse. Napoleon III, who had withdrawn his troops from protecting the Holy Father at Rome, was himself taken prisoner with 100,000 men in the Sedan. The French armies were paralyzed by the politicians of the republic which declared itself in power, while Prussia's overpowering armies of ten years' training in the art of "how to conquer the French" were passing from victory to victory. Gaston petitioned time and again to be sent to the front, but he was considered necessary in Africa. Most of the troops had been taken and it would have been an excellent opportunity for an insurrection. But Sonis had given such prestige to the French name that the disasters of 1870 did not shake the fidelity of the Arabian tribes. The pastor of Aumale remarked that perhaps the repeated refusals were the sign of God's will. Quick as a flash came the clear-cut answer: "Your advice would be decisive for me in an altogether different subject, Father. But when one's country is invaded, it is the duty of every soldier to ask to depart."

Théobald de Sonis was in the army at the Rhine, and Gaston's three eldest sons were at the front: Gaston, 19; Henri, 17; and Albert, only 15. It is necessary for commanders to set the example. On October 20, 1870, he received the grade of brigadier-general. On the capitulation of Metz, he telegraphed to Gambetta that if he was not recalled to France for active service he would give in his resignation as general and enlist for the front as volunteer, even as a simple soldier. Deeply impressed by such nobility, Gambetta confided to Sonis the 3rd Brigade of Cavalry provisionally cantoned at Blois. "I remember still his cry of joy on receiving this dispatch," recalled poor Madame de Sonis. "Alas! for me it was the beginning of dread apprehensions. It was the end of our beautiful and happy days."

De Sonis wrote: "A Dieu! I am marching to death. May

God have mercy on my soul, and take care of my wife and poor children. God may spare me, but an expiation is needed and He never capitulates, never!"

Disembarking at Marseilles, the general separated from his little tribe, first making the sign of the Cross on each forehead. They took the road to Castres while he went on to Tours. Sonis had left Africa never to return.

CHAPTER VIII

"Sunset and Evening Star"

On November 13, General de Sonis arrived at Tours, where the government had been transferred since the siege of Paris. He immediately presented himself at the War Office for information, but found confusion reigning. The next day, continuing his efforts to obtain information, he learned that he was named commandant of the 1st brigade of the 17th Corps' Cavalry Division. Where was this brigade, and of what was it composed? No one knew.

That same evening, November 14, he was given command, not of a brigade, but of a division, in the Army of the Loire. Where was this division? No one knew.

By the 16th he learned that he was under General d'Aurelle de Paladines, an able leader, and under the immediate orders of General Durrieu, with whom he had been on campaign in Africa. But where were his regiments? He was told to see if they were around Vendôme. At Vendôme there was no trace of the cavalry. See if they are at Châteaudun. There he found in the ruins of a half-burned town a squadron of cavalry. He ended by finding three regiments—mere trunks—of which he had to form his division.

During the night of November 17, he received the order

from General d'Aurelle to go to Fréteval, when General Fierreck asked his support at Dreux, where the Prussians were menacing. "You cannot abandon me!" No, Sonis would never abandon a comrade, but his orders were formal. He showed them to Fierreck and said if he did not have a response from d'Aurelle he would have to obey. No response came. His heart torn, Sonis left Châteaudun with his small brigade. Seeing the soldiers leave their town, the people cried out: "They are afraid of the Prussians!" They were soon scattered by Sonis who bounded on them, white with indignation.

At midnight the detachment reached Fréteval. The soldiers were watering their horses when the counter-order arrived: "Return to Châteaudun. Rejoin General Fierreck." Exhausted, the soldiers returned to Châteaudun to find that General Fierreck had gone to Mans. General Durrieu, likewise, was somewhere else. Sonis telegraphed to Tours:

"Who is Commander of the Corps stationed around Châteaudun?"

"You."

"For how long?"

"Act as if for always."

Was he dreaming? In a few hours he was promoted to general of a division, then general of an army corps. A telegram demoting him to the grade of simple soldier would have affected him less. He, a cavalry general, was put in command of territorial troops who hardly knew how to hold a rifle. The authorities knew in whose hands they were placing the honor of the country. Had they let go the military reins, perhaps the same hands would have led France victorious through the Franco-Prussian War. Sonis summed up the situation concisely in the dispatch sent to Tours:

"What the Army of the Loire precisely needs most is a corps of two or three divisions of cavalry disposing of ample horse artillery which could be used to harass the enemy and execute night raids as well as cut enemy telegraph lines, intercept railway communications and cut off enemy supplies in general, all of which would be of tremendous help. The many years I have spent on duty in South Algeria have given me a certain amount of experience in that type of action and I could be of value under such conditions. Instead of that, I have been given the command of an army corps that is poorly organized and with which everyone knows I cannot do much. The minister's reply directly engages my responsibility, however, and I must execute to the best of my ability the new duties I have been saddled with."

The First World War and the campaign into Russia in 1942 proved the truth of this principle.

Sonis spared no efforts to make the best of the materials he had. He worked day and night to gather his men, to form the Army of the Loire, to watch the movements of the enemy, to supervise countless details. The pastor of the church at Marboué, where the General made what he called his bivouac, found him one night stretched fully dressed on a wretched bed, the covers not even drawn up. "What, General! sleeping like this on so cold a night, in this damp room!" "Saint Louis never undressed when on campaign," answered Miles Christi.

There were capable and great leaders in that Army of the Loire, and noble, patriotic soldiers, whole regiments of them, but the armies and their chiefs were paralyzed by the civil powers retaining in their incompetent hands the military reins. The orders coming from Tours and the false reports given out (probably in good faith but through ignorance) crippled the armies and turned the events of the war in favor of the enemy. Brave and excellent generals were abruptly discharged while in full action and replaced by others—this for the sole offense of having obeyed too exactly the impracticable orders of Generalissimo Gambetta. The Prussians were doing all in their power to prevent the formation of the Army of the Loire, and to reorganize their own effectives, thrown back and disorganized by several victories on the part of the French.

On November 23, Vendôme was attacked. The French army was surrounded. Sonis was ordered to send at once to Vêndome two artillery batteries and an infantry brigade. He obeyed the order, but at the same time left his headquarters at Marboué with a light column to make a surprise attack on Brou. He hoped by attacking the left flank of the enemy to make them retrace their steps. On the march to Brou, Sonis discovered the difference between the troops he was leading and his magnificently trained troops of Africa. The men were marching through deluges of cold, penetrating rain, in snow, or in mire up to their ankles and often without the provisions that should have accompanied the troops—all for lack of organization. In spite of obstacles, Sonis arrived at a little village near Brou which they soon learned was an advanced position of the enemy. We can follow Sonis' report:

"The German fire was very heavy, but I had given orders not to return it for the time being in order to fool the enemy into thinking we had no artillery. When the combat was thoroughly engaged, however, I unmasked all my batteries and threw every gun into action in order to give the

Prussians the impression I had a large force. They apparently believed I had, for they withdrew from the field. I followed them to Brou, which they evacuated, and pursued them another two and a half miles. When night fell I pretended to bivouac there, then returned to Marboué, having accomplished all that I had set out to do."

The battle of Brou showed what can be accomplished by a capable leader and a handful of brave men. Fifteen thousand took part in the battle of Brou. Sonis had in his ranks the marines of Major Colet and the famous Papal Zouaves of Colonel de Charette. This victory forced the Prussians to retreat from two points, thus preserving the 17th Corps from being surrounded. A few more such initiatives would have saved the whole army.

The defeated Prussians lost no time in amassing their troops to regain lost territory. Sonis, who was fully aware of their movements, informed the other generals in that section and concluded: "I am here because I have been ordered to come here and my reply is that I shall remain here as long as possible. You can count on me." Of that everyone was fully confident. He prepared a stubborn resistance around Châteaudun and was planning an offensive attack when a thunderbolt arrived from Tours. He was ordered to retreat! The telegram was dated Tours, November 26, 4:25 p.m. It wrung tears of blood from the heart of Miles Christi. It was not military to discuss, to argue. He was a soldier; he obeyed. . . .

In the horrible gloom that was gathering over the Army of the Loire, a streak of sunshine fell across General de Sonis' path. The incident was told by Emile Fischer to Father Bessières when the latter was writing his life of the general in 1945. M. Fischer, a native of Africa, was then in his nineties.

"The 1st of December, my squadron was camped in a snow-covered field. Just at the moment we were preparing our horses to make a reconnaissance in the direction of Chartres, General de Sonis—that brave of the brave, that knight of olden days—passed the road bordering our bivouac. When he saw the Spahis with their red *burnous* (hooded Arabian cloak), he galloped up with joy and held out his hand to us native Africans. He had known us before when he was commandant of the Spahis. He asked some of us to be his escort and took us back with him at once to his headquarters. It was in this way that I became his pennon-bearer." The ensign General de Sonis had chosen was a white cross on blue background. He had wanted a crucifix, but it was painted so poorly that, artist that he was, he refused it for a simple cross.

During the night of November 29-30, Sonis was given the order to march; an attack was announced for the morrow. "The cannon will serve as guide."

"We were marching once again in the night." It is the General's report. "It was between 10 and 15 degrees. We advanced slowly over a broad and icy road. Our horses progressed with difficulty. Turning around to see who was following me, I saw Colonel de Charette who had just dismounted to warm himself by walking. I did the same and we began to converse together. We were soon joined by de Bouillé, de Cazenove, de Troussures, and Father Doussot, Dominican and chaplain to the Pontifical Zouaves. The conversation became very intimate. We spoke of the things of God. We were full of confidence. We felt we were going to fulfill a great duty. . . ." The names de Sonis records in this passage are written in blood across the brow of France, ever to be revered and remembered by anyone worthy of the name of French.

The Pontifical Zouaves were the soldiers who had fled to the protection of the Pope and the Papal States for which they had been fighting for ten years. When the walls of Rome were fired upon on September 19, 1870, Pope Pius IX ordered cease fire to prevent further bloodshed. The soldiers had to evacuate Italy. In October the 300 French Papal Zouaves rallied under their 38-year-old leader, Baron de Charette, as noble for his fearless courage and fiery patriotism as for his name. All the generals were eager to possess this elite troop, but Divine Providence gave them the chief most worthy to lead them—Gaston de Sonis.

When the general spoke with regret of not having a more religious standard, Coloned de Charette unfolded the following story.

At the request of certain holy and patriotic persons, the Visitandines of Paray-le-Monial made a banner, on the style of those carried in procession, to be sent to General Trochu so that it would float on the walls of Paris and protect the capital. The banner had to be made hastily as time was pressing. It was of white taffeta, about one and a half yards long by 24 inches wide. Standing out conspicuously in the center was a Sacred Heart surrounded by thorns. In red letters forming four lines was the invocation: *"Coeur de Jésus, sauvez la France."* Heart of Jesus, save France.

The way to Paris being blocked, the banner was sent to M. Dupont, the Holy Man of Tours, with the injunction to send it, if possible, to the defenders of the West. Having left Italy, Colonel de Charette was stopping at the same hotel as M. Dupont. They had mutual connections. Charette announced to his family that the government had accepted his Zouaves into the nation's army under the name of "Legion of Western Volunteers." Seeing the hand of God in this meeting, M. Dupont presented Charette with the banner of the Sacred Heart, before the picture of the Holy Face enshrined in his home. On the back of the banner he had the Carmelites embroider the invocation: "Saint Martin, Patron of France, pray for us." Then it was placed on the tomb of the Saint where it remained all night. A marble plaque in the crypt of Saint Martin of Tours commemorates this fact:

> "Here, the holy man of Tours, L. Dupont, laid the banner of the Sacred Heart, to be returned to Colonel de Charette and carried to battle at the head of the Western Volunteers under the orders of General de Sonis. 9 October 1870."

Enthusiastic over the history of the banner, General de Sonis immediately accepted it for his ensign and told the colonel to choose one of his men for standard-bearer. Charette designated Count de Bouillé, an intimate friend, but the latter declined, saying it was too great an honor for a laborer of the eleventh hour; the privilege should go to someone who had fought at Rome. He had only recently joined the Papal Zouaves.

Towards 11:30 p.m. the army reached an old château which de Sonis made his headquarters. He had Charette bring inside those Zouaves too young or delicate to remain out in such rigorous weather. Many soldiers were barefoot, marching through snow and ice. The supply wagon had lost its way. A fire was made and they supped lightly of bread, sausages and fruit. Colonel de Charette brought in Count de Verthamon and presented him to de Sonis: "General, behold your standard-bearer and here is your banner!" In the flicker of the fire's hungry flames, Sonis saw before him a fair and handsome young man. He had left his wife and two little children to go to the aid of the Holy Father. He was leaving them a second time to aid his beloved *Patrie*. He had begged Charette to consecrate publicly the Pontifical Zouaves to the Sacred Heart. Because of the skepticism of many, it was decided not to unfurl the banner until the cannons sounded. For the time being, it was rolled up and returned to its case.

The exhausted soldiers had only a few hours of sleep that night; Sonis had none. He had received a dispatch from General Chanzy begging him to lend one of his brigades; it was urgent. Sonis sent a brigade of the 2nd Division. Although so much in need of repose, the soldiers departed with eagerness. Sonis ordered General Deflandre to leave his post at once with the 3rd Division and join him at Patay. Patay . . . the field of battle where the Maid of Orleans carried her banner to victory! Doubtless, to be on ground sacred to all Frenchmen inspired hope and courage in the great leaders who knew they were facing almost certain defeat.

The day of immolation dawned. It was the 2nd of December, First Friday—the day consecrated to the Sacred Heart. The concise record drawn up by de Sonis, supplemented by the testimony of eye witnesses, will allow us to follow hour by hour the events of this tragic day immortal in French history.

At three in the morning, de Sonis woke his men and they assisted at the Mass of the Sacred Heart offered in the little church by Father Doussot. Many received Holy Communion which for them was to be Viaticum. After a short thanksgiving, Sonis gave the order to march toward Patay. He transmitted to his soldiers General d'Aurelle's order of the day: "Soldiers of the Army of the Loire! By a sublime effort of courage and patriotism, Paris has broken the

Prussian lines. General Ducrot at the head of his army marches toward you. Let us march toward him with the enthusiasm of which the Army of Paris gives us an example." This information given by Gambetta to the generals of the Army of the Loire was false. The last French resources were to be crushed against an impregnable wall.

Around 8 o'clock General de Sonis arrived at Patay, installed his troops and sent word immediately to Chanzy of his arrival, informing him at the same time of the absolute need of rest for his men. "He should not have come; a brigade would suffice to complete the victory," was Chanzy's reply, distractedly promising the requested repose. Intoxicated by his success the day before, General Chanzy departed at the head of the 16th to hurl his troops against an enemy far superior in numbers. He did not even wait until Sonis' Corps had been concentrated. Before long, General Chanzy was sending three messages, each successively more urgent, demanding immediate help from Sonis. Sonis did not let himself be annoyed by such conduct on the part of an officer of the same rank as himself and only saw in it the appeal of a comrade in battle. If he had any fault, it was that he judged others by his own degree of selflessness. Chanzy's troops were overrun and beginning to panic. His militia companies fled across the fields and Sonis tried in vain to stop them. Disregarding his own fatigue, Sonis saw to it that bread and hot soup were hastily issued to his exhausted troops. There was nothing left of his 17th Corps but a simple brigade; Chanzy had already borrowed one, the other two had been ordered to different points to attempt to divert the enemy's concentration.

Chanzy called again on Sonis, whom five hours before he had reproached for coming himself: "Please replace me here!" Assuming that Chanzy was planning to do what he would have done himself under such circumstances, i.e., regroup his men behind the thin screen formed by Sonis' brigade, then throw them into line again and relieve Sonis, the latter did not hesitate. Reluctant to censure a fellow officer, but not wanting to put the blame unjustly on his own men, Sonis said later that as soon as his men took over, Chanzy's battalions left the field altogether. "I could not have supposed I would not receive help, when I needed it. It was hard to think that after having come to the aid of an army corps I could no longer hope to receive help myself." The horrible reality shows up in these words. *Sonis was sacrificed by the one whom he had come to save.* There was one alternative: save himself by retreating, which would throw confusion into Chanzy's retreat; or, remain and be killed. Chanzy knew de Sonis; therefore, he must have known which he would choose. General de Sonis' tactics were to hold ground and attack, as were Marshal Foch's after him.

Leaving Deflandre's division in reserve with the order to "march to the cannon," General de Sonis marched on Loigny, while his artillery fired the enemy's position with admirable precision. "I would never know how to praise them enough," recorded de Sonis. It was the moment for Chanzy to bring back his troops to transform Sonis' success into victory.

Since four o'clock in the afternoon, General de Sonis had twice saved Chanzy's army, stopped two Prussian divisions, and inspired confidence in the two brave battalions commanded by Major de Fouchier who were holding their post at Loigny. To extricate them, retake Loigny, was to win the battle. Sonis prepared for the assault, ordered General Deflandre immediately to bring his division which was not far distant, and to come, "cost what it may."

101

At the very moment that General de Sonis was going to attack Loigny, he was informed that his center was falling back. It was the 51st Foot, a motley outfit thrown together barely a month before. Galloping towards them, he cried with all his force: "Forward! You are cowards, you will lose us, you are dishonoring us! Wretches, unworthy of the name of Frenchmen, I will brand the number of your regiment, I will blow out your brains!" Mounted on his horse, he was brandishing his sword in his right hand and shaking his cap in his left. Panic had seized the wretched men; they would not move forward. The Spahis of the general's escort struck them with the flat of their swords; they endured this outrage without advancing a step. Their cowardice was less to blame than their spirit. They had been conscripted, were without training, and were facing gunpowder for the first time. Many among them were brave men, but the superior command was poor. "It is good morale that makes good soldiers and a good commander is the one who creates good morale," was one of de Sonis' sayings.

Seeing his efforts useless, General de Sonis galloped back to his artillery reserve and cried to Charette for one of his two battalions. A cry of patriotism rose from those brave heroes, all so eager to die for their country. Sonis chose 300, leaving the others to guard the artillery, and gave the order: Unfurl the Banner of the Sacred Heart. . . . It could be seen from all parts. The soldiers kept their eyes on it. The effect was electrifying. Sonis made one last effort to save the demoralized regiment. "Soldiers! behold the flag of honor! Follow it! March!" There was a movement in the ranks only to fall back again. Fear is contagious; if it has followers, it means defeat. At all cost, panic had to be met by a noble example of courage. Then it was that de

Sonis made the heroic effort which, although it could not win the battle, saved honor and preserved two army corps from being annihilated.

General de Sonis advanced. At his right, on his large black horse, was Colonel de Charette, who had just finished his rosary. On his left, Major de Troussures, who threw himself on de Sonis' neck and said: "General, how good you are to lead us to such a feast!" These were to be his last recorded words. Father Doussot confessed some soldiers, then gave general absolution, section by section, holding his crucifix high above their heads. At de Sonis' side was Count de Verthamon bearing aloft the Banner of the Sacred Heart. The air was charged with patriotic and holy enthusiasm. It depended on them to save the honor of their country, their beloved *Patrie*. They marched forward with their battle-cry: "Vive la France! Vive Pie IX! Vive le Sacré-Coeur!" Such an heroic gesture on the part of the elite troop caused a movement forward in the paralyzed regiment, giving momentary hope; but facing fire, it retreated to abandon the fray for good. Remaining at the head of the Papal Zouaves, General de Sonis made a heroic charge on Loigny. He expected at any moment to be supported by Deflandre's 3rd Division. "Three hundred Zouaves thrust forward with me. I had destined them for one thing only: to produce a great moral effect capable of bringing a demoralized troop to its duty." Honor! For de Sonis that was far more important than victory. They charged through the woods with their bayonets, with such force and valor that the enemy, more than three times superior in number, fell back, thinking the little troop was the advance guard of a formidable army. The Zouaves pursued the retreating Prussians and were met by a fierce gunfire. Sergeant de Verthamon fell, a bullet through his chest. He rose and in a supreme effort carried the Banner forward until he fell again, this time not to rise. Count de Bouillé, who had humbly declined the privilege of standard-bearer, lifted the Banner on high. Suddenly it disappeared from sight. He, too, was shot down. Who would be the next target? His 26-year-old son, Jacques de Bouillé, was at his side. In turn, he lifted the Banner high and marched with such rapidity that it floated and flapped in the wind. He fell under fire, wounded many times. His body was never found. One after another, the lions of Charette tried to rescue the sacred Banner, now blood stained, but were shot down. A little Zouave, only 17 years old, crept behind the bodies of his fallen comrades until he reached the Banner, detached it from its staff and rolled it up. He crawled away, his right hand shot, but the precious emblem was safe. It was finally confided to Father Doussot, who had been no less heroic than the others during the whole of that magnificent charge. Conspicuous in his white Dominican habit, he held his Crucifix above his head, regardless of the bullets raining around him.

About 5 p.m., General de Sonis suddenly stopped his horse. A bullet shot from close range passed through his left thigh, shattering the bone. "It is finished for today," he said calmly to his aide-de-camp, whom he asked to help him dismount. Two officers lifted the general down from his horse, which was riddled with bullets. They laid him on the ground, put his saddle under his head and a cover over him. He was bathed in blood. They wanted to stay with him, but he sent them away with his order for the senior general officer to replace him in the command of the 17th Corps and to direct the retreat. He also sent by them his last messages and farewell to his wife and children.

Colonel de Charette's black horse reeled. The Zouaves

thought their chief's turn had come. No, it was the horse that was struck. Disengaging himself, Charette called to his Zouaves and fought on foot like a simple soldier, sabre in hand. They reached the first two houses of Loigny and took possession, fighting with stools and furniture when there was nothing else.

"All those who carried the banner of the Sacred Heart during the battle," recorded de Sonis, "fell wounded. It was the banner of martyrs. At the end of that unequal combat of 300 men against almost 2,000 Prussians, a Zouave took it from the hands of the last to fall and saved it, clasping it against his breast."

All the Prussian reserves were called into action and it was not until they had set fire to the houses that the Zouaves were forced to give up and Charette gave the signal to retreat. Time and again they would stop to turn back and fire once more on the enemy. The next day, a Prussian colonel said to Charette, injured and taken prisoner: "I have taken part in many battles, but I have never seen so magnificent a charge as that." Then he rose and gave him the military salute.

From the interior of the cemetery, Major de Fouchier continued to hold ground with the remnants of his 37th regiment. "Tell them to cease fire!" shouted the Prussian general. "That is not my affair, but yours!" came the fearless answer. At seven o'clock that night the survivors fired their last cartridge. The next morning their bodies were found frozen, standing against the cemetery wall.

* * * *

Chanzy, Chanzy, where were you? Why did you not return the aid that had been given to you so generously?

Oh, Deflandre! Why did you not come with your 10,000 men as you had been ordered—"cost what it may"? You died bravely in another battle at the head of your men, later on, but where were you that December day?

* * * *

Knowing that his artillery was saved and the advance of the enemy stopped, General de Sonis prepared for death. Later he could write of those under his command: "In finishing this report, I am happy to be able to state that the 17th Corps did not lose a single cannon during the time I had the honor of commanding it."

Before the parliamentary commission of inquiry, General de'Aurelle de Paladines bore witness to General de Sonis' action. "The 17th Corps had just been formed. It was composed of all sorts of men without military instruction, without organization. General de Sonis took command of this Corps in this condition. I must say that the short time he commanded it was nothing but an act of self-sacrifice on his part. Fired on by all sides, receiving contradictory orders which the administration dispatched to him, either from Tours or from some other quarter, he gave us heart-breaking details of the state of his troops. It was an act of great self-sacrifice to accept the command."

Perhaps this is the place to give General de Sonis' reply to those who thought he had yielded to impetuosity in leading the charge on Loigny, like some harebrained sub-lieutenant, while he should have saved himself for the sake of others. "I know what a sub-lieutenant should do and what a general should do. I was there because it was necessary to be there; march, no matter what, and die, if necessary, to prevent a greater disaster. I fell with those who had confidence in me and who followed me. I fell, but I did not lose a single cannon, and I saved honor."

Night fell over the battlefield. Death stole around in the frightful cold and touched one, then another, of those

Thermopylean heroes. Their holocaust was greater than those of ancient Greece because it was voluntary and it was Christian. General de Sonis was lying motionless and in agony under his cover. His blood was flowing profusely. The Prussian army passed over the bodies of the French, and soldier that he was, de Sonis could not help admiring the discipline of those troops. They stripped the bodies of what arms were useful, nor was the general excepted. Turning him over and back again with brutality, a Prussian removed his military belt, sword and pistol. He had to assist at the rejoicing of their victory, but the most horrible spectacle awaited him. A few feet in front and a little to his right, a Zouave injured in the leg, was lying, propped on his elbow. A Prussian went up to him, jolted him with his foot and finished him off by smashing his head with his rifle-butt. The victim was Major de Troussures who had thanked the general for sending them "to such a feast." Seeing another soldier coming directly toward him, de Sonis expected the same fate and commended his soul to his Master. "But that one was the good Samaritan. Having reached me, that man stopped, took my hand and shaking it in an indefinable gesture of goodness, said: 'Comrade!' Without doubt it was the only word in French he knew, but he put his whole heart into it. Leaning over me, this kind soldier tipped his flask and poured a few drops of brandy into my mouth. I had been fasting for 24 hours." He replaced de Sonis' head on the saddle and pulled the cover over him. Not knowing each other's language, the general thanked the good Bavarian by pointing to Heaven.

A Prussian medical corps removed their wounded. No offer having been made to de Sonis, he did not ask aid of the enemy. A German captain recorded that "they returned in the morning but there were no more wounded

French. All had frozen and were dead. The cold at 7:30 a.m. had dropped to 4 degrees below zero." A horse froze standing up.

"Soon silence fell around me," recorded Sonis, "silence broken only by the voice of the dying calling in vain for help. Never will I forget those heart-rending cries." He could see the silhouetted form of the Prussians as they warmed themselves passing to and fro before the blazing cottages of Loigny, now so many braziers. He could hear their harsh voices and triumphant laughter.

Around nine o'clock a prolonged cry announced help. Although he mustered all his strength to answer, de Sonis was not heard. He tried to drag himself in the direction of the voice but found himself incapable of movement. The voice faded farther into the distance. Suddenly two men bearing a lantern appeared only fifty paces away. "General, we are going to be picked up!" cried the wounded around de Sonis. Their voices were too weak to be heard. De Sonis recognized the voice of one of the two men. It was a priest of Limoges he had known as a seminarian; he had volunteered as chaplain to the troops of Haute-Vienne. He saw the priest and his companion leaning over the bodies lying in the snow. Thinking all the injured had been removed, they departed for the improvised hospital where 240 wounded awaited them.

The darkness deepened with the increasing silence as the moans of the agonizing faded into death. Over the general's sepulchral form nature was spreading her pure winding sheet of snow, gently but surely. He made a vow that night to the Sacred Heart that if God spared his life he would spend the night of December 2-3 every year before the Blessed Sacrament.

Around eleven o'clock, two young Zouaves dragged themselves to the general's side and asked him to speak to them of God. "We were on the threshold of those ever-lasting hopes which form the prize, as it were, of this great battle which we call life. On this threshold the Church has placed Mary, so as to inspire confidence in those who are about to cross it. The Immaculate Virgin was, therefore, the subject of my conversation with those two young men."

All the skin had been shot off the forehead of one of them. After a time, they felt they could attempt to reach the next village, so after bidding good-bye to the general they departed, supporting each other. They were taken prisoners before reaching the village.

Another young Zouave dragged himself over the snow to the general and leaned his head against de Sonis' left shoulder. He died shortly afterwards, calling for his mother.

The snow continued to fall in large flakes. The silence of death shrouded the field of carnage. Miles Christi had comforted and strengthened others. Was there no one to solace his last hours? His soul was plunged in mortal sadness as he thought of the anguish his death was going to cause his heroic wife and the little tribe dependent on him. He was leaving her with ten children; the oldest only 20, the youngest under 2, and she was not yet 40. Were his three sons in eternity or still fighting for *la Patrie* . . . or something worse? Did he know that Albert, who belonged to the 16th Corps, had been fighting only some 100 yards from him?

Miles Christi had always been a loving son. When a child dies, the mother is sure to be at his side; nothing can keep a mother from her boy when he is in trouble. In the gloom of darkness, a Star appeared that starless night over the blood-soaked battlefield and shone over where the Soldier of Christ lay. Our Lady of Lourdes appeared to General de Sonis that night on the battlefield of Loigny.

"She did not leave me. Before the war I had made a pilgrimage to the miraculous grotto. From that time I have always pictured the Sacred Virgin as in that statue of Lourdes. I can say that this sweet image was constantly present to me during the whole night that I passed on that bloody soil where I awaited death during long hours. Thanks to Our Lady, those hours, although long, were not without consolations. My sufferings then were felt so slightly that I do not even remember them."

In her cell at Carmel, Mother Marie-Thérèse was suddenly awakened by a voice: "Get up and pray. Someone belonging to you is suffering." An unseen hand seemed to urge her up and she called out: "Who is there?" thinking it one of the Community. Receiving no answer, she began to pray. Five of her immediate family were at the front: two brothers and three nephews. Her beloved Gaston seemed to have a charmed life. The Sacred Heart would protect him for the sake of his children. It must be the boy Albert. She prayed through that unforgettable night in her icy cell. The next day General Chanzy's dispatch on the battle of Loigny, contained this phrase: "I still do not know what has happened to General de Sonis."

To return to Sonis' account: "The snow continued to fall and my blood to run, but without suffering. I had always before me Our Lady of Lourdes, and I felt a peace, an ineffable interior consolation. I did not begin to suffer until men concerned themselves about me."

Near five o'clock in the morning two Prussians went up to the general, but noticing his eyes open, they did not touch him. They took the arms, some of the clothing and the money of the young Zouave who had died on his shoulder.

Two hours later French voices were heard, but they

withdrew without noticing Sonis whose calls for help were too weak to be heard.

The brandy was burning his chest and so devouring was the thirst that he believed death inevitable. " 'My God, I commend my soul into Your hands.' Then I invoked Mary conceived without sin. In spirit I beheld the image of the White Virgin of Lourdes and in place of seeing death come, I felt succored."

Around ten o'clock voices were heard again, this time quite close. The general called for help several times, and waved his right arm, the only one free. The gesture was seen by the chaplain of the troops of Mayenne. He rushed up to the general who said he had come just in time to prepare him for death. "Oh, no, general. Let us hope your wound is not mortal!" It took two interminable hours to procure a stretcher. Hearing the word "general" the Prussians lent one, but sent an officer along to bring it back in fifteen minutes, timed by their watch. De Sonis endured excruciating torments when he was lifted, for not only was he severely wounded, but partly frozen and covered with snow and ice. All along the way, at each jolt which renewed the agony, he murmured: "O my Master! my good Master! You suffered more than I." It was noon of Saturday, December 3. The General had lain there since five o'clock the preceding evening.

The rectory, transformed into a hospital, was the destination. The pastor gave up his own bed to the general. "It seems to me I can still see the good general on his arrival," the pastor recorded. "He was pale as death; his head and clothing were covered with snow and frost. . . . It was necessary to cut the whole length of the boot from his wounded leg. Then he was put on the bed in my room where there was a good fire. It was not for several hours,

111

when he had returned a little to himself, he noticed, besides the wound in his left leg, that the right foot was frozen." His blood drenched the mattress and seeped through, congealing on the floor.

On Sunday, December 4, Dr. Dujardin-Beaumetz declared an amputation necessary. "Try to leave enough so that I can still ride a horse and serve France," came the general's reply.

The amputation took place that night around eight o'clock by candlelight. The bone had been splintered into twenty-five fragments. Under the chloroform, the general continued to pray and to give orders to his soldiers while the surgeon sawed and carved.

Thus was written, in blood, an immortal page of French history.

CHAPTER IX

Sacred This Soil

~~~~~~

"While they carved, and sawed and cut," recorded de Sonis, "I felt nothing. But afterwards! For 45 days I suffered till I was almost out of my mind. I could not sleep one minute during the whole of that time. The tick of the clock alone became a veritable torture, so weak was my head. Yet I must bless God who knows how to draw our good even from our evils. The bleeding caused by the amputation cured me of an inflammation of the lungs contracted in the snow which the doctors did not think could be cured.

"Dr. Dujardin-Beaumetz returned to see me the next morning. I told him I could not feel my right foot. The foot had frozen and gangrene set in. He scraped out everything that was infected. This was another frightful torture." This time no anaesthetic was used.

One of the first things the general did after his arrival at the rectory was to ask for a Mass for the German soldier who had shown him kindness on the battlefield.

On December 8, Feast of his Immaculate Mother, Mass was celebrated in the little room adjoining, and de Sonis received his Master. The priest was the chaplain, the former seminarist of Limoges, who had come so near to rescuing the soldier of Christ that night on the battlefield. After Mass he told the general he had asked for his complete rehabilitation and promised to go Lourdes if his prayer was heard. De Sonis answered: "I asked for perfect conformity of my will with the adorable Will of God. Our Lady of Lourdes! Ah, yes! We must go there. If you knew how She helped me. Believe me, I do not regret you let me pass the night out there."

The general was not forgetful of his duties as chief. He dictated a full report for the War Office. It ended: "Although I have lost my leg in practically the whole length, I am too old a cavalier not to hope, as soon as rehabilitated, to be able to put myself at your disposal and still serve my country." A chaplain told him he had written to Madame de Sonis. The general thanked him and said: "Ah, if she knew of my condition and where I am, nothing would stop here from coming, even if she had to come by balloon!"

* * * *

And what was Madame de Sonis doing during the immolation of her husband—immolation that was offered for the beloved *Patrie?* On reading General Chanzy's bulletin: "I still do not know was has happened to General de Sonis," she telegraphed the War Office. Not waiting for the reply, she went to Tours where she was misinformed. From town to village, from village to city, in a borrowed and wretched cart, she traversed enemy-infested territory bearing all the horrid marks of war. On December 23, after nineteen days of anguish, through snow and cold, Madame de Sonis reached Loigny. "I did not dare to ask if my husband was still alive. I found him at last, but in what condition, O my God! I would have passed through fire to reach his side, had that been necessary." Passing the bodies still unburied and the arms and legs heaped up outside the church, passing through the 2,000 wounded soldiers packed into the little church where the air was charged with the odor of dead flesh and blood, the valiant little woman finally reached the general's side. Oh, the pathos of that meeting! "My poor child, what are you going to do here?" he murmured. Suffer with him, console him, wrestle with death. Little Anaïs, you were worthy to be the woman of his love!

Madame de Sonis slept on the floor beside her husband, sharing the cold and all the privations of those hard days. The Germans had taken all the provisions; Loigny was in charred ruins, and often there was nothing to quench feverish thirst but stale water and melted snow. The pastor who had given up his room and moved down to the cellar contracted frightful rheumatism. Nevertheless, he spent himself begging provisions from other villages. The surgeons continued their operations; arms and legs were strewn about and blood was everywhere.

Everyone went to General de Sonis for strength in his pain, for spiritual uplift, for courage to face life crippled or helpless from then on, or to prepare for the eternal meeting above. "The martyr of Loigny," as he was called, was the admiration of everyone, even unbelievers. When his own sufferings gave him a brief respite, he would have his wife read a chapter of the Gospels or of *The Imitation*. All went to him to gain courage to make the sacrifice demanded of them. Colonel de Charette, that lion of France, hobbling on his injured leg, was among those who visited the general. "It is impossible to pass a quarter of an hour with General de Sonis without leaving his presence a better soldier and a better Christian," was his comment.

A few hours after de Sonis arrived at the rectory, Henri de Verthamon was brought in. He had lain on the battlefield for twenty-four hours before he was discovered. He was to endure his passion next to Miles Christi. It lasted three days. His two mortal wounds caused atrocious suffering. To the nursing sister caring for him, he recounted the charge. Standard-bearer, he was in the lead, flourishing the precious Banner. "We all knew we were marching to death; to me it seemed like going up to Heaven. It was sublime!" The priest considered it the "greatest joy of his ministry" to assist him. Never had he witnessed such generosity in suffering. After receiving the Last Sacraments, de Verthamon asked for his crucifix and the photograph of his wife and two children (a third was expected). "One of my children will never know his father, but God will take care. Tell them all that I love them tenderly and will love them in Heaven. . . ! I have only one sacrifice to make to God, that of my family. I offer Him this sacrifice with my whole heart!" Kissing the crucifix, he murmured "Jesus, Mary, Joseph." The "saint of the regiment," as he was called, had fought his last fight; his short course was finished. Learning of his death, Colonel de Charette said: "It is permitted his friends to weep for him, but also to envy him!"

Then there was Lucien Saulnier, the little Zouave who had an arm and foot cut off. General and Madame de Sonis recited their rosary during the operation. Lucien had asked only one thing of God: to see his mother again before he died. Madame Saulnier did learn of his whereabouts and came to care for him in the little rectory. "I went to the general's bedside," she said, "to draw the strength and courage necessary not to succumb. After seeing his sufferings and hearing his words I would return to my dear child and impart to him the spiritual strength I drew from the general." Lucien entreated her: "Mother, let me die! You are stopping me from going to Heaven. I beg you, let me die!" The beautiful statues of the Sacred Heart, Our

116

Lady and St. Joseph in the Memorial Chapel are Madame de Saulnier's gift.

The atmosphere of the rectory was overcharged with the odor of blood and human flesh, to which was added tobacco fumes—the soldiers' only diversion. No one suspected the suffering this caused General de Sonis because of his bronchial congestion. Colonel de Charette was not the least offender, puffing pipe after pipe as he sat by the general's bedside. The doctor feared for his patient and intervened. The fiery Charette limped off fuming, this time not with tobacco, but with impatience at his lack of consideration for his friend.

On January 28, General de Sonis was transported to better quarters in the covered vehicle the Little Sisters of the Poor at Chartres used for their begging tours. The Marquis and Marchioness de Gouvion-Saint-Cyr turned their château into a hospital and offered the general and his wife hospitality. At that time it would have taken six or seven hours to reach the château, which is in the direction of Chartres. They remained there over a month. A maid in the service of the household recorded the edifying remembrance de Sonis left behind: "Very often the general had himself carried to the Chapel to receive Holy Communion; he was taken down also to the large hall where most of the wounded were. There he would say a kind and encouraging word to each one. In spite of all his sufferings, there was so much peace and resignation in his face that one could not help admiring him."

Before leaving the environs of Loigny, at the beginning of March, General de Sonis visited the battlefield once more. He conceived the desire to erect a cross over the spot where he lay for twenty hours that unforgettable night. He joined the committee that was formed to undertake the restoration of the old church and to build in it an

117

ossuary for the heroes fallen in battle, but in his humility he refused the title of president. That title, he said, belonged to Charette.

This is indeed holy ground, soil soaked in blood. Every year on December 2, the Bishop of Chartres presides at a ceremony which commemorates the epic-making events of that day. A procession forms in the church and files out to the very sites we have been tracing. It is now a ploughed beet field. There you will see the cross of stone marking the spot where the general lay. There is the slab marking the grave of Major de Troussures, who died under the blows a Prussian dealt him on the head—a cruelty suffered by other soldiers. A white statue of the Sacred Heart on a tall stone pedestal reminds the visitor that these heroes fell under His Banner. In the old cemetery a granite column commemorates Major de Fouchier and his heroic men.

The church, dedicated to the Sacred Heart, was built as a memorial to the Battle of December 2, 1870. In it are two very fine paintings, the work of a Zouave who fought in the battle. To the right of the altar, at the Epistle side, is the "Communion of the Zouaves." General de Sonis is receiving the Blessed Sacrament from Father Doussot. At his right is Major de Troussures; the artist of the picture is holding a candle. The fair-bearded Charette is standing behind and receiving the Banner of the Sacred Heart from an angel who holds in his other hand the cup of sacrifice.

On the left, at the Gospel side of the Altar, is the "Agony of Sonis." There you will see the general stretched out, his head on his saddle, a cover over him. His gaze is fixed on the white figure of Our Lady of Lourdes above, who is extending her arms towards him. Fernand de Ferron has come to die on his left shoulder. At a little distance is

118

Major de Troussures being clubbed to death. In the background the village of Loigny is in flames, the church standing intact.

The hanging lamps in the nave and the choir are made of souvenirs of the battle: small chains from the equipment, helmet spikes, Prussian eagles, bayonets. Above is a Prussian shell. On the benches traces of blood are still visible.

In the crypt of the church you will see behind an iron grille two tombs. One is marked with the simple words: MILES CHRISTI—General Gaston de Sonis—and his dates. The other: Charette, 1832-1911. CREDO.

Sharing together their funeral couch, these great Frenchmen seem like two lions sleeping in their den, ready to spring forth to the defense of their country. A marble slab reminds the visitor that Madame de Sonis is buried under her husband's tomb.

Between the tombs and above, in a glass case, is the Banner of the Sacred Heart still bearing the traces of blood. Opposite is the ossuary containing the skulls and bones, quite visible through the glass covering, of the some 1,200 combatants fallen in the battle. A beautifully executed medallion of a slain Lamb dominates this awesome sight.

On December 2, 1956, the Bishop of Chartres blessed the *musée* adjoining the church, which owes its origin to the indefatigable pastor. The museum was constructed to contain the relics and souvenirs of the martyrs of Loigny, and to accommodate the ever-increasing number of pilgrims. In breaking ground for this museum, the foundation of the old rectory of 1870 was struck, making it possible to locate the pastor's room and the actual site of the bed where General de Sonis suffered for forty-five days till he was almost crazed with pain. By a happy coincidence, it is just behind the present statue of Saint Thérèse of the Child Jesus.

Among the souvenirs in glass cases are instruments of penance used by the general, the boots he wore December 2, 1870, the left one cut the whole length, garments, French and German arms. Mention must be made of two dented bugles; they were used to sound the immortal charge—a charge heard only by the gallant . . . de Sonis, de Fouchier and their men.

Loigny is a small and sleepy village approximately 79 miles southwest of Paris and is easily reached in two hours by car. Leave Paris via the Porte d'Orléans and follow Route Nationale 20 for 96 kilometres (60 miles) to Artenay, then turn right off the highway to Patay and continue to Loigny which is only 31 kilometres (19 miles) from Artenay. Route Nationale 20 is a magnificent main highway. The road from Artenay to Loigny is a secondary one which does not figure on the majority of maps, but like practically all French roads, it is in excellent condition.

Loigny can also be reached by taking the train to Chartres or Orléans and completing the trip by bus. Loigny is approximately midway between the two cities.

Such sacrifice for Christ Jesus and for honor never dies but will live on forever in a nation. To many the Battle of Loigny was a useless immolation. To the same eyes Our Lord was a failure. But let us not forget that it was on the eve of His great "failure" that Christ said: "Have confidence; I have overcome the world." It is Truth Who is speaking. Loigny has a lesson even for us in America, first and foremost for the soldier, but for every private citizen as well: human success is not the important thing. We must do our utmost even in the face of defeat. Honor, Duty—these first.

CHAPTER X

The Royal Road

~~~~~~

Sonis did not die. Loigny was only the beginning of his *via dolorosa*. For seventeen years he had to drag a broken body along a road that grew constantly rougher and steeper. He who had meditated for years on *The Imitation of Christ* knew he "could not find a higher way above, nor a safer way below, than the way of the Holy Cross." The years of shadow when twilight came at noon revealed even more astonishing heroism than the brilliant chivalry of youthful years.

General de Sonis visited Lourdes and left at the miraculous Grotto as ex-voto offerings his first crutches and the cross of Commander of the Legion of Honor, which he received after the Battle of Loigny. He remained all day at the Grotto, communing with his Immaculate Mother. He obtained the cure of his youngest son, François, still suffering from fevers contracted in Africa, and for himself, perfect resignation to his state. He made many visits to Lourdes during the remaining years. Silence was the only answer to the outpourings of his heart to his White Virgin of Lourdes who kept the secret of the graces She caused to flow into his soul.

The General and wife arrived at Castres, where their

children were waiting for them. Gaston, Henri, and Albert had distinguished themselves in the army and were decorated.

When the term of his leave of absence was drawing to a close, he offered his services at the War Office. "What position do you ask?" "I ask only to serve my country." Sonis' life blazed one straight trail . . . no byways, no vacillating. It is living on the surface, like butterflies flitting from flower to flower, that causes so much want of stability today.

Sonis asked to serve as colonel, since he had been promoted on the battlefield. Such a petition had been addressed to the War Office only once before, and that by Charette who had been made general after the Battle of Loigny. It is to Sonis' glory that the Commission of revision of grades granted him *unanimously* the rank of general of division.

In October, 1871, the government placed Sonis at the head of the 16th military division, which took him to Rennes, Brittany, where he remained until 1874. There was another reason for assigning this post to a man of de Sonis' mettle. It was feared the Breton coast might tempt Napoleon III who had taken refuge in England, as Napoleon I had escaped from Elba. Five Departments were under his jurisdiction. During the three years that Sonis remained at Rennes, he worked at the material and moral reorganization of the Army. He used to say: "It is the manly virtues of discipline and self-sacrifice which give an army the strength to win battles. Fortresses may be built, new arms forged and clever tactics adopted, but the main strength of an army will always lie in its morale."

He was revered by the citizens of the town for his kindness to the poor, his courtesy, his long visits to the Blessed

Sacrament. They had only to look at him to know how the saints pray, as Saint Thérèse said of her father. Every Saturday saw him mingling with the common people to make his hour of prayer as member of the Perpetual Adoration Society. Every month he was faithful to the meetings of the Third Order of Carmel. Two attendants would assist the General into his place and there he would remain during the instruction with recollection that impressed all who saw him. Although so great a master of himself, de Sonis could not always hide the evidence of graces passing through his soul at the holy words the director addressed to the tertiaries. The director, a Discalced Carmelite Father, testified that the general was the recipient of graces so great he could not sustain their weight. Fearless in battle, de Sonis would tremble in church, so conscious was he of the presence of God. Every year he spent the night of December 2 in the Carmelite Chapel. After confessing, he would remain alone before the tabernacle. He would receive Holy Communion at the first Mass in the morning, then go directly to his office and start his day's work. Asked once if he was not tired after staying up all night, he answered: "Tired? after a night on watch!" He turned and went off, the tap of his wooden leg sounding down the stairs.

He was bound by the Rule of the Third Order of Carmel to strive for the perfect accomplishment of the duties of his state. To this end he gave several hours a day to studying military theories. He astonished the other officers by his knowledge of the least details. With the simplicity of a child he would have an officer listen to him recite what he had learned. He never dispensed himself from the multiple annoying little duties that usually are left to someone else or left undone. In this respect he was remarkable.

De Sonis had had fashioned a complicated apparatus

making it possible for him to ride the horse again. A hook on the side of the saddle secured his thigh, while a leather boot received the wooden leg. He had to be hoisted up on the stump and pass his right leg over his horse. He could not repress involuntary cries of pain each time he was lifted into the saddle, but once mounted, he would thrust the peg leg into the boot, which was supported by the stirrup. Seeing him racing at the head of his troops, riding the most spirited horses, in the saddle ten and twelve hours at a time, no one suspected the physical torture he endured in silence for sixteen years. An idea of his sufferings can be gathered from this letter: "I have persevered in riding, which is necessary for my inspections. Yesterday, my wooden leg broke, and remained sticking in the stirrup. I was galloping at the time, and the broken wood dangling against my horse's legs might easily have caused a bad accident. But, thank God, I was able to stop him, and to reach home in safety, though very tired by the efforts I had to make to keep my balance."

An officer of his staff has left this description of General de Sonis at this time:

"Under his gentle exterior and his invariable courtesy, his soul was inflexible as regarded duty, and made him often appear severe in his inspections. His height and his dignified manner inspired respect and a certain amount of fear in those who saw him for the first time. But, in reality this apparent austerity was assumed to conceal his natural kindness. His personal integrity and disinterestedness were well known." Gaston de Sonis was very handsome, with singularly aristocratic features, dark hair and moustache and dark brown deep-set eyes. He admired and loved nobility of soul and uprightness of character. He remained young at heart and loved to refresh himself with the officers

124

of the future, especially the tertiaries of Carmel, his "brothers in Jesus." Political or religious considerations never influenced him in the classification of the officers. A soldier was to be advanced on merit alone. When asked to use his influence to promote someone, he would refuse saying he had never solicited anything for himself or for his own. When the commission sat to consider the classification of one belonging to him, he would be absent. A priest asked him to spare a young soldier, his protégé, the lack of privacy of the barracks. "I believe a true Christian should not fear difficulties when God imposes them. He has His views and the presence of a pious young man in a barrack room can do more good than one supposes." He promised, however, to do what he could to have the young man placed under a good colonel.

A colonel wanted to be promoted to brigadier-general; he had to settle his daughters in life. Sonis bounded. "To marry his daughters! What a reason for becoming general! To marry his daughters!" he muttered, "to marry his daughters!"

In his opinion, a person who was influenced by human respect was cowardly; therefore it was doubly out of place in the soldier. He insisted upon his men being treated with consideration and humanity, and he used often to say: "It is as cowardly to abuse one's authority over inferiors as it is to flatter superiors."

He was inflexible in forbidding duels within the territory under his jurisdiction. The civil law as well as the Church forbade them. A colonel told a soldier to settle a dispute by a duel. The soldier, overcome with fright, fled from the field. Learning of the affair, General de Sonis imprisoned the colonel a week for ordering the duel, and the soldier a month for giving way to fear. "Are you not afraid of compromising yourself?" he was asked. "Compromise myself? Thank God, it is a long time since I gave up caring about that!"

In October, 1872, Marie, the oldest child, entered the Society of the Sacred Heart at Rennes. She had become the comfort and right hand of her parents. They made the sacrifice generously, but it was no less keenly felt. On leaving her at the convent, her father said: "Be a holy religious; if you are humble of heart, you will be." Marie made her novitiate at Conflans near Paris. Her parents were present at her reception of the habit on February 2nd, Feast of the Purification. She had no better guide than her incomparable father whose letters form precious spiritual direction. "Be Marie of Jesus for time and for eternity," he told her. Nor were the general's directions confined to letters. The exterior of a religion, as of a soldier, must denote the order within. One time the novice greeted her parents with her headdress in disorder and wearing an apron. The general told her she was not at the barracks and sent her back to arrange herself properly. Another time she opened the door to them too hurriedly. "On what are you making your particular examen? Abruptness, I suppose?" The novices had been discussing the greatest heroism in life. Marie asked her father's opinion and received this answer:

"I believe that true heroism consists in constant fidelity to the humble and hidden way. Love the place where you are not noticed. Be happy when, lost in the rank and file, you feel you are counted for nothing. Then only do you walk in a glory that lights the soul without burning it." No comment would be worthy of such clear-visioned spirituality.

Mother Marie de Sonis made her profession in August 1880, at which her parents were present. "Always walk in the way of perfection," her father told her. "Your efforts will be a blessing for your whole family." She suffered from poor health. "You know, dear child, how easy it is for you, in sickness, to draw near to Jesus, your Divine Model. In that state, the soul has only to submit to the will of God. Our Lord willed to take the figure of a lamb, always gentle and submissive under the knife of sacrifice. He loves with predilection those who are submissive to Him in sickness."

It was a comfort to know that the lessons he had taught his little girl under the starry skies of Africa were refreshed in her mind each time she recited the words in the Office: *"Coeli enarrant gloriam Dei,"* "The heavens shew forth the glory of God" *(Ps. 18.)* It was a particular consolation to the soldier that his daughter was a member of the Congregation consecrated to the Heart of Jesus under whose Banner it was his privilege and honor to do battle and to fall. Mother Marie de Sonis died in 1928. She was at the convent of the Sacred Heart in Poitiers the last years of her life. The Spanish lay-sister, Josefa Menendez, was receiving the revelations of the Sacred Heart at that time. The General's daughter was, therefore, among those of whom Our Lord said such consoling things. "I am much loved here. . . . This house is the garden of My delights. I come here to seek consolation when sinners offend Me and make Me suffer. Tell them that I am indeed the Master of this dwelling, that it is a beloved refuge to Me and that My Heart finds rest in it. I do not want or ask for great things. What I want, what is a consolation to Me is to find love that prompts good works, and that I find in this house."

Seven months after making the sacrifice of his "first born," the Master called home another Marie dearly loved. On May 31, 1873, the general's youngest sister, Mother Marie of the Blessed Sacrament, died suddenly at the Carmel of Poitiers. Twenty years before, on the same day, she had entered the Carmel. Her lively and ardent nature had much to suffer, and one day her saintly brother said to her: "My little sister, it seems to me that when one has given one's self completely to such a Master, one can refuse Him nothing thereafter." She gave herself entirely from that time forth, wishing to keep nothing that did not belong to her Master alone. She spent that last anniversary of her entrance to Carmel in joy, recalling the graces she had re-received. In the evening, she said to her Sisters: "It seems to me my time is finished; there is nothing more but to die." She returned to her cell after Matins, around eleven o'clock at night, and was suddenly seized with pain. The chaplain was summoned immediately and she died peacefully while receiving the Last Sacraments. The general made the diffi-cult journey from Rennes to Poitiers, and in the same place where he had assisted at her Clothing in the Habit of Our Lady, he kept vigil before the grille until ten o'clock at night. The smile with which Mother Marie of the Blessed Sacrament had passed through the sufferings of her whole life was still on her countenance. The general returned at four o'clock in the morning, and after assisting at the Masses celebrated in the chapel for the repose of his sister's soul, he went to the door of the enclosure to meet her last remains. Thinking it more perfect that no exception be made and fearing the emotion would be too great for his brother, he declined the Prioress' offer to open the coffin. Sacrificing an ardent desire to embrace his sister for the last time, he contented himself with kissing the rough wood that enclosed her.

It was an impressive sight to see the rough, plain coffin of the humble Carmelite carried to the cemetery of the town where her sisters in religion lay buried. It was escorted by the priests and religious of the city, her two brothers—generals—by all the civil and military authorities, and a detachment from the garrison, as well as a cortege of the highest personages of Poitiers and its environs.

"Behold one life less: but behold one more happy eternity!" Miles Christi inherited the rosary of his little sister, whom he "tried to replace at the feet of Mary Immaculate."

As the anti-clerical attitude of the government grew more pronounced, pilgrimages multiplied and General de Sonis took part as often as his condition allowed. The one held at Paray-le-Monial in June, 1873, was the most celebrated. Twenty-five thousand Communions were distributed; nine hundred and fifty banners represented the provinces and cities of France. The Papal Zouaves were there with General de Charette and the torn, blood-stained Banner of the Sacred Heart. It was the first time that many had seen the Soldier of Christ since Loigny. There was a vast difference between the aged and infirm soldier and the leader of the heroic charge. However, a cord of one of the banners was put in his hand and he held it to the end of the procession. His wound opened and blood was trickling down. Charette came up to support him under the arm and the crowd could no longer restrain itself. "Vive Sonis! Vive Charette!" rang through the dense throng. "No, no!" cried de Sonis in his voice of command, "Cry: 'Vive Jésus!' "

The Cross bore down on the Soldier of Christ until, like the Master, he was one with it. The general was thrown from his horse and broke his only leg. For forty days he suffered excruciating pain and for four months was unable to walk. After two months of helplessness, the doctors discovered that a bone in the hip was fractured and they applied a plaster cast. His patience and resignation edified all who came in contact with him. The priest who brought him Holy Communion said he was more than a saint—Sonis was an angel. Had the remark been made to him, he could have answered in the words of St. Thérèse when, ten years

129

later, a similar remark was made to her: "No, I am not an angel; angels cannot suffer." He had a new apparatus made and to the astonishment of his doctors rode his horse again. Seeing him at the maneuvers, no one could suspect the tortures he endured.

He offered his physical sufferings for the Church and for the cure of his poor country whose pitiable condition weighed more heavily on the Soldier of Christ than did his own pains. His loyalty to the Church was known to everyone. He was branded "disciple of Loyola" by those whose descendants in our day called General Weygand "in the pocket of priests." Such people reveal themselves out of their own mouths. The general made no secret of being a royalist. Those in high places gave the preference to their followers, and de Sonis expected at any time to be thrust from his post. It was a crucifying preoccupation for a father of ten children. His virtue was tried in the testing fire of humiliations and proved true gold. In spite of his condition, he had to submit to five displacements before the end.

From 1874 to 1880 he was stationed at Saint-Servan where he and his family occupied a villa called "Amélia" which had a lovely garden. His elder sister, Mother Marie-Thérese of Jesus, was lent by the Carmel of Poitiers to the Carmel of Coutances, recently founded from the Carmel of Lisieux. The general's courses of inspection took him within the locality of the Carmel where he would stop. These visits could be likened to the conversations between Saint Teresa of Jesus and Saint John of the Cross, so spiritual were they. "Nothing less than submission to the Rule could separate us," declared the general. Confiding to her brother her *"cupio dissolvi et esse cum Christo,"* (her desire to be dissolved and to be with Christ), Mother Marie-Thérèse was reproved. "How can a daughter of Saint Teresa wish to die to cease to suffer?" He opened the horizon of living longer to make more sacrifices for the love of God, to which she agreed he was right. Spiritual literature has lost, perhaps, some of its most beautiful pages in the destruction of the correspondence between these two great souls. It was at the general's express command that all his letters be collected and destroyed. He declared that to share them would be a betrayal of his friendship, so intimate were they.

Mother Marie-Thérèse died as prioress of the Carmel of Coutances on November 22, 1875, only two and a half years after her younger sister. It was during the novena preparatory to the feast of Saint John of the Cross. She gave her last blessing to her sisters who surrounded her bed. She had passed "24 years of prayer and immolation in Carmel." In her, General de Sonis lost a mother, a sister, his most intimate friend and confidante. Owing to a false movement of his wooden leg while leaving the house to attend her funeral, he was unable to be present. His brother Théobald replaced him, while he was nailed to his bed in an agony of pain. In his last letter to her, which she was to read in Heaven, he had written: "From afar I embrace you tenderly, while offering Our Lord the sacrifice of your holy cloister which deprives me of the happiness of sitting by your bed and holding your hand, as I hold your heart in mine." When Gaston de Sonis loved, it was with the intensity of a Frenchman and the heart of a saint.

Saint-Servan is the cradle of the Little Sisters of the Poor. Although the general's own means were so restricted, he never turned a Little Sister from his door. It was his delight to pass his free time among the "old folk," encouraging them with his holy words and doing what he could to assist them from his wheelchair. The work of the Little Sisters was after his own great heart and he could never admire them enough.

A Judas was not wanting to the passion of Miles Christi. A man who owed much to General de Sonis was responsible, or largely responsible, for the rude and humiliating removal from command that occurred in March, 1880. Moreover, the expense was enormous for the always too thin purse. De Sonis and his family were loved and venerated by the Bretons in whom the Catholic faith is so deep-rooted. Gaston and Henri had chosen wives from among the old nobility. His younger children were settled at schools there. The anti-clericals thought the "disciple of Loyola" would resign from the Army rather than accept the disgrace of this displacement. He was bullied and ragged in the press for hanging on. One of the Rogatory Processes for the beatification of the Servant of God took place in Brittany, at Rennes.

De Sonis was sent to Châteauroux which brought him under the command of General Marquis de Gallifet, a man of high military distinction but of different religious calibre. His unexpected and annoying inspections were the dread of his subordinates. Before entering into his territory, de Sonis wrote to Gallifet to say he feared that he would not find him active enough. The response was worthy of a true superior general: "Do me the favor of having the same confidence in me that I have in you. . . . Do not disturb yourself by coming to see me. . . . Moreover, I count on going shortly to Châteauroux, but not for an inspection. I esteem you too much not to have complete confidence in you and I do not count on making any inspection in your division." At the union of the generals under him, de Gallifet made de Sonis, despite his protests, sit in his own chair, that of president. "Your services and our respect give you the first place here," Gallifet said. "I know no officer superior to General de Sonis." General de Gallifet imprisoned for 30 days an officer who wrote an article ridiculing the crippled soldier of Loigny. "No one knows better than he how perfectly to command and perfectly to obey" was General de Gallifet's testimony of Gaston de Sonis. It was due to Gallifet's intervention that the general was made Grand Officer of the Legion of Honor in June, 1880. Sonis had refused to sign the request according to custom, not wanting to seem to solicit a favor of a government that persecuted the Church. His emblem of Grand Officer of the Legion of Honor was piously kept by the Carmelites of Verdun, until November 11, 1956, when it was presented by the grandson of his name to Saumur National Cavalry School at a splendid ceremony held in his honor. It will be remembered that General de Sonis graduated from Saumur as sub-lieutenant to the 5th Hussars in 1848.

The general had been at Châteauroux only three months when the storm broke. The decree ordering the dispersion of congregations of male religious was executed by force. The blow fell first, as usual, on the Jesuits; a few months later it fell on all the other congregations. The Army and the police force were called in to aid in the abominable act. Many refused or resigned from their posts. Others shut themselves up in the houses with the religious to protect them. Tyrannous authority will always find hirelings—a certain class, a certain type—ready to carry out odious commands.

Sonis had a friend at the Benedictine Abbey of Solesmes. Dom Sarlat felt he owed his vocation to a conversation he had with Sonis one starlit night in the port of Algiers. He was then captain of a frigate and had distinguished himself in many battles. When, on November 5, 1880, a commisary of police and soldiers entered his cell to take him by force, the Benedictine monk became again the former captain. The wretched men fell back and, in spite of themselves,

133

saluted the commanding figure standing before them, his Benedictine scapular studded, for the occasion, with all the decorations he had received for defending his country. As he marched out, he was showered with flowers and hailed with the *vivas* of a dense throng.

When the order came for his troops to participate in the expulsion of the religious, General de Sonis sent in his resignation. "In selecting the military career," he wrote, "I was willing to make the sacrifice of my life, but not of my honor. If I have nothing else to give my children when I die, I want at least to leave them a name that is honored and respected." General de Gallifet multiplied his protests: "General, I cannot grant your request; you are the honor of the Army."

In November, 1880, General de Sonis was relieved of active duty. He advised other officers who wanted to follow his example: "Do not desert the Army. Remain at your post until *non licet,* until it no longer honorable to do so.Be willing to be dragged before a council of war and to lose your life rather than disobey God. All that is very simple and very clear. I have always been of the opinion that we should remain at our post until *non licet.* To leave would simply be helping the enemy. Had I not been of this principle, I would have left the Army long ago. I did not withdraw until the day my soldiers were forced, by higher order, to be employed for a sacrilegious work. It was then that I was faced with *non licet,* and I did what you know. Believe me, it was not without tearing my heart that I left the Army." To another: "Do you tell me you are leaving the Army on your wife's advice? She has no grace to give counsel in such a matter."

The lords of torture chambers know that a victim who can hold out against their inhuman inventions over months and even years will break down when someone he loves is tortured in his presence. The general's wife and children shared the humiliations and poverty subsequent to his retirement. They had to leave the general's headquarters to take up residence in a miserable hovel where they were crowded one against another. He passed to the ranks in the same town where before he had enjoyed first place. The small pension did not take into consideration his large family. "Providence will not abandon me. I have become accustomed to miracles. God will perform one rather than abandon me." Sonis had not long to wait.

General de Gallifet worked to have de Sonis given active service where politics could not interfere. In May, 1881, the War Office named him general inspector of cavalry with Limoges for residence. The new position was all the more pleasing to the general, as in case of war it would call him to the frontiers at the head of a cavalry corps of four brigades.

Gaston de Sonis was anticipating the return to Limoges, so full of happy memories and the home of Louis de Sèze and Henry Lamy de la Chapelle and his friends of the Saint Vincent de Paul Conference. Henri Lamy was asked to procure a house within the modest means of the de Sonis family. But all the streams of the general's affections were to be dried up to draw him more purely to his Christ—the Source. Like candles snuffed out by an unseen hand, his closest friends died one after the other. The great Cardinal Pie went to his eternal reward only two days after Sonis had paid him a visit. It was a holy bond that joined in close, understanding friendship the son of the noble families of de Bébian and de Sonis with the son of the Parisian shoemaker who became a Prince of the Church. On what ground do the levelers of class stand in the face of such nobility?

Count Louis de Sèze, who was the grandson of the lawyer

who defended King Louis XVI, died after weeks of intense suffering. His passing was felt keenly by his faithful friend, Gaston de Sonis. Only four months later it was Henri Lamy de la Chapelle. The de Sonis family had visited them the day before. His death was sudden, and in him the general lost his best and closest friend. His death broke the last link formed at Juilly. Sonis' letters to Henri's widow are sobs from a broken heart. Oh, the tenderness and the fidelity of the heart of a saint! How blessed are they who experience it!

The people of Limoges gave de Sonis a warm welcome. He was loved and revered as their "saint," but the "martyr of Loigny" was a far cry from the lieutenant of twenty-eight years before. Where now was the brilliant cavalier with the dash and valor that fascinated the Arabs, those master horsemen? The same energy and courage remained in the flash of those dark eyes, but they had taken on a softness and depth from years of contemplating the Heart of the Master while growing into His likeness. "No one hath so lively a feeling of the passion of Christ as he who hath happened to suffer such like things," says *The Imitation*. (Bk. II, Ch. 12). It was sorrow rather than time which lined the face of Miles Christi as the sun of his popularity sank behind the hill of oblivion.

In spite of his physical condition, the general took up his work with invincible energy. Ten and twelve hours in the saddle, inspecting the cavalry divisions, passing from city to city, he was active from four in the morning until seven in the evening when he would retire to his room to bathe the wound the wooden leg kept open. At the field maneuvers in September he was thrown from his horse and broke the wooden leg. Two days later he was back on the horse and terminated the maneuvers. He never recovered completely from this terrible accident and lost confidence in riding the horse. He developed a horror of what had become second nature to him. With death in his heart, he asked to be retired from the Army. The answer arrived in January, 1883. "Since the war I have not ceased to walk a downward path. . . . God be blest for mingling me more and more with the little ones for whom I have always had great attraction. God has given me the grace to love more, to practise better every day, the sweet and charming virtue of humility, of which He was the incomparable Exemplar during his mortal life."

General de Sonis finished his life in Paris, the City of Lights, and the capital of his country. His last residence was in the quartier de l'Etoile near the Church of Saint-Honoré d'Eylau. He was appointed member of a commission of Public Works at the War Office: "A situation of no importance which in our military language is termed burial of the first class," was his comment. He had to attend a monthly union of the members to study projects of fortification. This left him much free time, which he devoted willingly to his God and to his children. He was little more than a living trunk of humanity. For weeks he would be huddled in his armchair, helpless. The wound of the amputation never healed and there were times when it was impossible to use the wooden leg or to walk on the other. Abscesses formed on the wound and had to be cauterized. Methods in those days were crude, nor were there any pain-killers. He suffered a veritable martyrdom from nerve pains that shot up his leg from the foot that had been frozen. He nearly died from the intensity of the pain alone. The bronchial congestion contracted from lying all night in the snow was with him to the end.

Although crucified in his body, tortured in his mind by anxiety for his family, and in anguish over the condition of his country, it must not be imagined that de Sonis was a gloomy influence on his surroundings. His patience and resignation were the admiration of all who came in contact with him. The Carmelite Fathers who assisted him in these last years looked on their visits as a pilgrimage and went away renewed in fervor to spend themselves in their ministry. He retained his gaiety through all his sorrows, never losing the sparkle of his French wit. Desiring to discuss some matters with him, the President of the Republic invited the general to dinner. It was Friday; meat was served. Noticing that the general was not eating, the president was profuse in embarrassed apologies and soundly reproached his wife for forgetting that it was Friday. Sonis was much amused by the transfer, as old as Adam, of the blame to the woman. Another time, the troops marched by for inspection. Contrary to his express orders, the supply wagons were in front. "French Army!" he shouted, furious at being disobeyed, "You are an army of the stomach! To the rear!"

Although so strict a disciplinarian, with his children he was even more tender than their mother. Germaine was fourteen, a sensitive age tempting to big brothers' desire to tease. She began to cry. "Oh, Germaine, don't cry over such a trifle," said Madame de Sonis. The general beckoned to his little daughter, pressed her head on his shoulder and caressed her hair in a way that was all his own. "Don't cry, now; you are my consolation," he said softly to her. This incident was to remain Germaine's consolation throughout her long and laborious life. He had such horror of anything false that he would not tolerate even childish fibs in his children. His spiritual mother, the great Saint Teresa, who saw so clearly that God is Truth, would not let her daughters use even trivial exaggerations to make their stories at recreation more entertaining to their sisters. In his last letter to his son Henri, the general planned that they meet in Brittany, and added: "Don't let Françoise (Henri's wife) forget to bring her ball dresses." Perhaps an unexpected stroke from one so disciplined, if we forget that the saints have big and understanding hearts, also that God wants to share our joys and smiles as well as our sorrows and tears. The letter was dated August 1, 1887.

Two weeks later the general seemed so much weaker that Madame de Sonis summoned the doctor. She wanted to call her sons who were absent, but the doctor assured her there was no cause for alarm. Around six the next morning suffocation began and hope was lost. The general's Carmelite confessor brought him Holy Viaticum and administered the last rites of the Church. Madame de Sonis held her Gaston's hand during the whole of the terrible agony that lasted eight hours. At two o'clock the struggle was over. Before closing his eyes, the general gazed at an invisible object in a transport of joy. . . . Had the Vision of Loigny returned to be his Morning Star at the dawn of Eternity? It was Monday, August 15, 1887, Feast of the Assumption, feast par excellence by which the French nation is consecrated to Our Lady. Immediately after death, General Gaston de Sonis' features took on a transfigured appearance.

The funeral took place from the church of Saint-Honoré d'Eylau, which proved too small to accommodate the throng that crowded around the bier: seven generals, Papal Zouaves, soldiers, priests, religious, and friends. The general's six sons, three in uniform, carried the holy remains, followed by his brother, General Théobald de Sonis. His daughters accompanied his wife, heroic to the end. In accordance with her husband's wish to be buried as a poor man and without military honors—in protest to a recent decree forbidding the troops to enter the churches—Madame de Sonis refused the guard of honor which had to remain outside. After the Mass and the last absolution, the coffin was set down on the threshold while General Lhotte, delegate of the Secretary of War and President of the Cavalry Commission, pronounced these words in a voice broken with emotion:

". . . The life of General de Sonis is too well known for there to be need to retrace it here. He was the model of all the military virtues as well as of the virtues of private life. The word duty written on the front page of his life is found throughout.

"Good-bye, General de Sonis! Good-bye, glorious soldier! You will remain among us as a great model which we shall try to approach, but without hope of ever attaining, so great were your virtues.

"Once again, Adieu, or rather, in my Christian faith, I say to you: Au revoir!"

The body of General de Sonis was taken to Loigny for interment. People from all over France were crowding the little church which was draped in black. The pillars were decorated with the de Sonis coat-of-arms and flags commemorating the battles in which the General had fought: Solferino, Morocco, Metlili, Ain-Madhi, Brou, Loigny. The same pastor was there who had so heroically served the wounded seventeen years before. General de Charette was present, surrounded by a large number of his Zouaves. He who would share his tomb in the same crypt with Miles Christi said: *Non sum dignus*. No, I am not worthy to go and rest near that saint, unless he carries me up to Heaven, as he drew me across the battlefield." The magnificent funeral oration, delivered by the Bishop of Angers, closed with the following words of hope and expectation, which since have proved prophetic:

"Henceforth, when we wish to seek for lessons of the most sublime patriotism, it is to Loigny that we shall come, by the side of this tomb, so glorious a memorial of French bravery and Christian faith. It will be a pilgrimage for all who value devotedness to duty and the rarest military virtues. I do not know whether, at the prayer of faith, God will deign to work miracles in this ever-blessed spot. I do not know if the Church, always desirous of glorifying the chosen souls among her children, may not some day bring into still more vivid light a life in which the noblest Christian virtues were practised even to heroism. But what public veneration permits me now to affirm without fear, is, that the memory of General de Sonis will remain through generations upon generations, surrounded with the respect and veneration of all, for he was truly great, before God and before men."

CHAPTER XI

The Answer

~~~~~~

The story of this book opened with a question: *Quis es tu?* Who art thou? This brought before our minds the Precursor of the Lord. When Saint John the Baptist sent disciples to Christ to ask if He were the Messiah or were they to look for another, Our Lord did not answer them in so many words. He detained them for a few days, let them witness His manner of life and His miracles. Then He sent them back to their master with the injunction to tell what they had seen and heard. The same has been done to our kind reader. You have been detained a few hours over these pages. In them you have found the answer to the opening question.

And the Soldier's Message?

General de Sonis is a model of the virtues most needed to combat predominant evils today. As we have seen, he belonged to the Order of Mount Carmel. The spirit of Elias the Prophet, Founder and Leader of the Carmelites, lived again in him. It was fitting, then, that our story should open with the Precursor in whom was the "spirit and power of Elias." "How long do you halt between two sides? If the Lord be God, follow Him." *(III Kings, Ch. 18, v. 21)* "As the Lord of hosts liveth, before whose face I stand. . . ." *(Ibid. v. 15)*

The invading powers of materialism break against such spirit. He who saw so distinctly the root of the evils of his day which brought down to the dust the faded glory of the past of his beloved country, is no less clear-visioned now. Honor, duty—these two words are stamped on every page of his life. Unfortunately, Adolf Hitler was not alone in considering a contract "just a piece of paper." Do we not need the example and the intercession of one who never yielded to that insidious influence of "everybody does it"?

The Order of Carmel has for specific aim to pray for the needs of the Church, the Sovereign Pontiff, priests, and for souls. We have seen how impregnated with this spirit was General de Sonis. This intrepid soldier of Christ will keep guard over His Vicar on earth threatened by enemies on all sides. "If I am general," he said, "it is to protect the rights of the Church in the Army." And we have seen how he envied those who could give their life to protect the Sovereign Pontiff.

When Charette and his Zouaves publicly consecrated themselves to the Sacred Heart on Pentecost Sunday in 1871, they used the prayer composed for the occasion by General de Sonis whose infirmities prevented him from being present. Of this consecration, Blessed Pius IX said, on presenting the church at Loigny with a gold ciborium: "The Zouaves have more effectively served France and the Church by the banner of the Sacred Heart and their public consecration than by the sword."

To the widow of General Théobald de Sonis on pilgrimage to Rome, Pope Leo XIII said: "Sonis! how much this name means to us. Sonis fought a good fight. He served well, both the Church and his country. He may be counted among the blessed."

In the Religious Orders of the Church the priests and brothers from the First Order, the cloistered nuns the Second Order. The Third Order consists of persons living in the world who are desirous of a more perfect form of life and who strive for the perfection of their state according to the spirit and under the guidance of the Religious Order to which they belong.

The Third Order of Mount Carmel was canonically erected in 1452. After St. Teresa established her Reform of Discalced Friars and Nuns, the Teresian Third Order, with its loftier spiritual doctrine and more austere rules, came into existence. It is known as the Third Secular Order of the Blessed Virgin Mary of Mount Carmel and of the Holy Mother Saint Teresa of Jesus; it is the strictest of the Third Orders. Its purpose is to allow persons living in the world to enter into the spiritual family of Carmel and share more fully in the treasure of spiritual riches of this glorious and ancient Order that Our Blessed Lady has been pleased to call Her own. The Habit which the members wear day and night is a scapular of brown wool cloth worn under one's clothing. The tertiaries take the vow of Obedience to the Superiors of the Order and the vow of Chastity according to one's state in life. Besides Mass and Holy Communion they are supposed to say daily the Little Office of Our Lady and make one half hour of prayer. In Europe this Third Order is flourishing with members both men and women of all professions and states in life—from cardinals and bishops to humble office employees. Less well known in this country it is, however, enjoying a steady increase in membership.

General de Sonis joined the Third Order of Mount Carmel on

144

October 15, 1862, the feast of the great Reformer of Carmel —St. Teresa of Jesus. He was unable to make his profession a year later, as is customary, his military obligations detaining him in Africa. His form of Profession, made at the house of the Discalced Carmelite Fathers at Bordeaux on August 27, 1869, is preserved at the Carmel of Verdun. In honor of the Poverello, the immortal troubadour of his Lady Poverty, and for a more complete dedication to the Master he loved above all things, he took the name of Brother Francis of Jesus. It was through heroic fidelity to his duties as tertiary, from which he never dispensed himself even on campaign, that General de Sonis attained such heights of sanctity. He was happy that the last move of his military career took him to Paris where he could benefit by the direction of the Carmelite Fathers who attended him to his death—a duty they looked upon as an honor and a privilege for the Order.

After the death of General de Sonis, the following prayer was found among his papers. As it is a resumé of his interior life we give it in full:

"My God, behold I stand before Thee, needy, little, bereft of everything.

"I am nothing, I have nothing, I can do nothing.

"I am here at Thy feet sunk in my nothingness.

"I wish I had something to offer Thee, but I am nothing but poverty.

"Thou art my All, Thou art my riches!

"My God, I thank Thee for having wanted me to be nothing before Thee; I love my humiliation, my nothingness.

"I thank Thee for having withdrawn from me some satisfactions of self-love, some consolations of the heart.

"I thank Thee for the disappointments, injustices, anxieties and humiliations of my life. I realize I had need of them and that these good things could have drawn me from thee.

"O my God, be Thou blest when Thou provest me. I love to be broken, consumed, destroyed by Thee. Annihilate me more and more.

"May I be to the edifice, not like the stone worked and polished by the hand of the artificer, but like the grain of sand, hidden as the dust of the street.

"My God, I thank Thee for having disclosed to me the sweetness of Thy consolations, but I also thank Thee for having taken it away. All that Thou doest is just and good. I praise Thee in my spiritual poverty. I regret nothing except not having loved Thee enough. I desire nothing but that Thy Will be done.

"Thou art my Master and I am Thy property. Turn me about. Destroy and work me. I want to be reduced to nothingness for Thy love.

"O Jesus! how good art Thou even in the severest trial. Would that I were crucified, but crucified by thee. Amen"

It was this prayer that inspired Saint Thérèse of the Child Jesus with her thoughts that have immortalized the little "grain of sand." In October 1887, Father Pichon, S.J. preached a retreat to the Carmelites of Lisieux, during the course of which he spoke about this prayer of the General, recently deceased. Saint Thérèse kept a copy of it in her prayerbook. There are references to the "grain of sand" in notes that Mother Agnes of Jesus and Saint Thérèse wrote to each other, and the expression became a community byword in the Carmel of Lisieux.

When Cardinal Pacelli, now gloriously reigning as Pope Pius XII, was sent to Lisieux as Papal Legate for the

146

Blessing and Inauguration of the Basilica in 1937, he united in one prayer the words Saint Thérèse wrote for her Profession: "Lord Jesus, grant that no one may think of me, that I may be ground under foot, forgotten, like the grain of sand," and the prayer of General de Sonis that inspired them: "Lord, that I may be to the edifice, not like the stone worked and polished by the hand of the artificer, but like the grain of sand hidden as the dust of the street."

Sanctity is not the usual companion of the soldier, although the sacrifices of the military career are as fertile soil for growth in holiness. General de Sonis is the exemplar of every man in uniform regardless of race or nation. "He loved the Army, to which he gave forty years of his life and all his strength and all his sons; and for which he strove to procure every glory and every virtue." (Mgr. Baunard) Following his example would produce the knight of the chivalrous days of yore.

Monsignor Gay said of him: "Such a man does honor to his country and his century. Certainly, France has the right to be proud of him; the Church even more so, because it was in the doctrine that she preaches, in the holy laws that she sets forth, in the gentle and strong piety that she inspires, that the General found the secret to be what he was. I speak of honor, that is not enough: Creatures whom God possesses to such a degree are a gain for the society in which they live, and one does not share so practically in the immolations of Jesus Christ without becoming, like Him and with Him, a saviour of the people."

We may ask ourselves: what was the source of the greatness in this man of marked character, of his courage not to compromise his convictions, of the breadth and length and height and depth of his love whose overflowing embraced the Church, the Army, Christians, Moslems—in a word, everyone? There is only one answer: the Sacred Heart of his Master, Christ Jesus.

The story of General de Sonis' life is the story of a man in love with God, of a man in love with a woman. It is only fitting that a few words be said about the valiant companion of our hero. Madame de Sonis survived her husband by 40 years. When Gaston was dedicating himself more completely to God, Anaïs looked on with disapproval. She feared she was being pushed out of that tender heart with whom she was in love. She was a woman, she was a wife; she could stand no more of it. With shame, she admitted she was jealous of God! Gaston, deeply moved, then showed her how groundless were her fears and how a heart can love yet deeper when freed of human attachment. Thereafter, Anaïs, generous and noble of soul as she was, strove to follow closely in her husband's steps. During the last years of the General's life she joined the Third Order of Mount Carmel, taking the name of Sister Teresa of the Sacred Heart. She made her Profession on July 16, 1884. It was the happiness of the general and his wife to say together the Little Office of Our Lady. After his death, until the end of her life, Madame de Sonis used his Tertiary Manual to read her Office. She who followed her husband to the utmost of her ability in his military peregrinations spent the years after his death striving to follow him in his climb heavenward. The end came gently on January 21 of the year 1927 when Madame de Sonis had reached the age of 96.

Gaston and Anaïs de Sonis are models for married life. But it may be asked what became of the children of such exemplary parents? What did ther faither leave them, since he was always poor? He left them a pattern of life which rust cannot consume nor the moth destroy. He left them

148

one of the greatest and noblest names in France—because his greatness was in his humility; and his nobility was in his loyalty to his Crucified Master. "He fought the good fight, he kept the faith." Perhaps it will be consoling to most parents to know that some of his children were just ordinary Christians. Unfortunately, sanctity is not hereditary! Of his daughters, only one married; Philomena, the Benjamin. Jean received a fatal injury to his knee in an accident on the horse while practising at the military academy. His leg was amputated when he was twenty-five and he died soon after. The general was in Eternity, so was spared this final cross. François, the youngest son, was a child of three when his father fell at Loigny. He used to play horse with the wooden leg. He, too, would be a general when he grew up . . . but not with a peg leg! He died in 1942 at the age of 76.

We have already seen Henri, the second son, asking his father's permission to join the Papal Zouaves, when he was only fourteen. He was the son most like the father and became a brilliant officer. He resigned from the Army rather than take part in the expulsion of the Religious in 1904. A group of officers went to the Cardinal of Rennes for advice when it became evident that their regiment would be used to aid in expelling the Religious. "Officers, you can march without incurring any responsibility. Your departure would be a loss to the Army; and then there are your families, the future of your children." Major Henri de Sonis rose: "Your Eminence, my comrades can march. I, with the name I bear, cannot." General Gaston de Sonis lived again in this son. Henri was true to the word he promised his father when only seventeen: "I take before you the solemn pledge of never failing, even once, in my duties as a Christian and a man of honor." He died a pious death on Palm Sunday in 1936, at the age of eighty-three.

General de Sonis would have been proud of the grandson bearing his name, a son of Henri, who volunteered for the colors in the First World War when he was fourteen years old. He was wounded and returned decorated. He was present at the general's exhumation. At the ceremony held at Saumur on November 11, 1956, he presented the Cavalry School with his grandfather's emblem of Grand Officer of the Legion of Honor and other souvenirs. He stood at the head of the troops and made the presentation while the band gave a flourish of trumpets. A stack of rifles had been arranged and the articles placed on them. The graduating class of 1956 which was given the name of "SONIS" then marched by. There was a solemn moment at the War Memorial, followed by a Mass sung by the officers. This impressive ceremony illustrates the undying influence that Gaston de Sonis has on the Army he served so gloriously.*

---

* Following is the allocution General de Clerck gave on this occasion:

"Cavalry Reserve Student Officers:

"Before departing on an assignment which prevents me from being here at Saumur when you leave at the end of the month, I want to say farewell to you, and to christen your class.

"In a solemn ceremony this day, I have received for Saumur, where he entered as 2nd lieutenant in October 1846, the emblem of Grand Officer of the Legion of Honor of General de Sonis; this presentation is made in the presence of his family and descendants. I wish to thank them for this gift which enriches our museum of relics, for we now possess something belonging to a man who during his entire life was an honor to our Army.

"This is a time when the majority of the nation is giving a magnificent example to preserve our fathers' work in Africa, while a minority gives itself over to criticize. Remember that before he was the hero of Loigny, this great patriot was for 16 years the great soldier of Africa, whom the Arabs called "Moula el Dinne"—the Just one.

"I cannot do better than quote, 70 years later, the words of one of my most illustrious predecessors among the commandants of Saumur, General Lhotte, who was called to speak before the mortal remains of his venerated chief:

'From the first to the last page of the book of his life was written the word "duty"; this book is now closed today. General de Sonis is the model of every military virtue as well as of every personal virtue; he remains the example to which we all must aspire, even without hope of ever equalling.'

"Reserve Officers of the Class 'SONIS', could there be a finer name to confer upon you, who unite the past with the future?"

We shall mention only in passing, Yves de Sonis, a grandson of Henri, who died in 1934 when he was nine years old. The inspector of free education made him a heavenly patron of all the children confided to his care, and of him his valiant mother wrote that she felt impelled to join to her sorrow a deep thanksgiving for the privilege of having possessed so pure and charming a soul for nine and a half years.

It was the tenth child, Germaine, who resembled the general the most in character and appearance and who seems to have inherited the largest share of his indomitable energy and depth of spirituality. She was only four and a half when her father fell on the battlefield of Loigny, and she grew up at his side learning how the saints suffer. He called her his consolation, his "aide-de-camp," and it was on her arm that he leaned as he went early every morning to Mass. She confided to him her desire to be a Carmelite, but she did not enter until after his death. As it was her saintly father who gave her her name in baptism, Carmel did not change it, so Germaine de Sonis became Germaine de Jésus when she changed her white bridal gown of rich satin for the rough undyed *bure* of Saint Teresa's Reform. One year later she received the Black Veil, at which ceremony the great Charette was present with the blood-stained Banner of Loigny. Also present was the Carmelite Father, Augustine of Jesus Crucified, the general's last confessor. It was a day of splendor for the austere chapel of Carmel, and a day of poignant memories for the bride of Christ. She was later elected prioress and founded the Carmel of Verdun, where the Nuns have the special obligation to pray in perpetuity for those fallen in the War of 1914-1918.

Mother Germaine had a presentiment that her father's body was preserved from decay. She quietly prepared a new uniform, regardless of the discouragement generously given. When the tailor asked that the general for whom he was making the trousers be brought in for a fitting, he received this disconcerting answer from the nephew charged with the negotiations: "Impossible. My grandfather has been dead 42 years."

In view of the process for beatification, the body of the general was exhumed on September 26, 1929. Mother Germaine was present in her white mantle. When the coffins of lead and wood were opened, and the winding sheet unfolded, there lay General Gaston de Sonis in a state of perfect preservation, clothed in the livery of France and of the Mother of God; his tertiary scapular was over his uniform. His body had not been embalmed and the crypt was damp. As Mother Germaine kept vigil all night by his remains, he seemed the same as on his death bed. Before the tomb was closed again, Father Augustine put his own scapular on him, and Mother Germaine placed in his hands her Profession Crucifix, taking back to her monastery the tertiary scapular that had been in the tomb for 42 years. Her Nuns noticed that her face was transfigured; she went about like one preoccupied with another world. Mother Germaine of Jesus is undoubtedly one of the great Prioresses of Carmel that France has given the Order in our century. One of her sayings was: "Tell God that you love Him, then prove that you do; there is the whole life of a Carmelite." During the Second World War the Nuns were obliged to leave their monastery. They took refuge in Lyons. Mother Germaine was 74 when she had to flee before the Germans. The intrepid little woman bore under her Carmelite habit her father's sword. After a short absence, she returned to her monastery, where she and her Nuns remained during the Allied bombings. Her confidence that her father, *"le bon papa"* of the Community, would protect her Carmel and her Nuns was fully rewarded. She died on Christmas Eve, 1945, aged 79, being the last of the twelve children born to General and Madame de Sonis to join them in Heaven. Her life, as interesting as it is edifying, was written three years ago by André Trannoy and is already in its third printing. It can be obtained at the Carmel of Verdun.

And so, on they march, in uniforms of God and of country, and in the livery of men and women in the world. . . .

Live again, great soldier of France, live again in your descendants, for the world has need of you; live again in your vast family of Carmel, in the men and women who are

153

striving to fill the place God has appointed them in the world. Help us to "labor as good soldiers of Christ Jesus" in bearing aloft the standard of your ideals so well symbolized by the blood-stained and torn Banner of Loigny, because they were taught to you by the Sacred Heart of Jesus. As we strive to march in the path you traced, which is none other than to follow the bloody footprints of the Master, may we never surrender those ideals of honor and duty, so that the Master you loved so passionately may some day recognize in each of us a reflection of

Miles Christi!

* * * * * *

The pen would have to be dipped in the Heart of the Master to write worthily of His servant. . . .

In thankfulness for extending your hand when other human hands were withheld, I lay these unworthy pages at your feet, *Miles Christi,* so that they may be presented to our Mother Immaculate through your noble hands, with a humble prayer that some . . . be it but a tiny drop . . . of the blood that flowed in your great heart may beat in mine "till the Day break, and the shadows retire!"

PRAYER TO THE SACRED HEART OF JESUS

(For the Beatification of General Gaston de Sonis)

Sacred Heart of Jesus, Thou whom General de Sonis served so faithfully on this earth;

Thou, whose Statue held the place of honor in his home and to whom he listened during his frequent Communions and his long visits to the Blessed Sacrament;

Thou, the cause of his tender devotion to Mary and Joseph;

Thou, his model in his love of poverty, his Guide in comforting the poor and the unhappy;

Thou, the source of his filial attachment and respectful submission to the Holy Father and to the Church;

Thou, the Inspirer of his zeal for the salvation of souls and for all noble causes;

Thou, whose devout soldier he wished to be and actually was, in Society and in the Army;

Thou, his strength in battles, his support in adversity, his consolation in sufferings;

We beseech thee to hasten the Beatification of Thy worthy servant, to give him the gift of miracles; to grant this prayer so that we may have recourse to him in our difficulties, in our pains, in our maladies, that he may intercede in our favor.

Amen.

Imprimatur—May 17, 1956
✠ James A. McNulty
Bishop of Paterson

155

Bibliography

LE GENERAL DE SONIS, d'après ses papiers et sa correspondance, par Mgr. Baunard, Paris, Librairie Ch. Poussielgue, rue Cassette, 15. (Out of print)

SONIS, 1825-1887, d'après de nombreux documents inédits, par Albert Bessières, S.J. Beauchesne et ses Fils, Paris, rue de Rennes, 117. 1946. (Out of print)

LE GENERAL DE SONIS par Jean des Marets. Fernand Sorlot Le Monde Catholique, 21, rue Servandoni, Paris, 1934.

SONIS—LOIGNY par M. le Curé de Loigny-la-Bataille, Introduction par le Général Weygand. 1955.

GERMAINE DE SONIS par André Trannoy. Editions Alsatia Paris. 17, rue Cassette. 1954.